"Pat Shapiro's new book, *Heart to Heart: Deepening Women's Friendships at Midlife*, is a wonderful blend of the author's own experiences, original interviews with married and single women at midlife, as well as highlights of pertinent secondary research. Her well-written book offers practical suggestions about how to improve friendship at midlife at the same time that it shares inspirational anecdotes and examples."

—JAN YAGER, Ph.D., sociologist and author of *Friendshifts®: The Power of Friendship and How It Shapes Our Lives*

"A vibrant midlife experience for women includes deepening friendships, observes Pat Shapiro in her compelling book *Heart to Heart*. In fact, women often prefer the company of their friends to their husbands. If you find this shocking, read on! I learned a lot about myself and my friends."

—PAULA P. HARDIN, Ed.D., Midlife Consulting Services, Chicago, and author of *What Are You Doing with the Rest of Your Life?*, *Love After Love*, and *Stages of Loving*

Heart to Heart

Deepening
Women's Friendships
at Midlife

Patricia Gottlieb Shapiro

BERKLEY BOOKS, NEW YORK

A Berkley Book
Published by The Berkley Publishing Group
A division of Penguin Putnam Inc.
375 Hudson Street
New York, New York 10014

Copyright © 2001 by Patricia Gottlieb Shapiro
Book design by Tiffany Kukec
Cover design by Erika Fusari
Cover photograph by Kamil Vojnar

PRINTING HISTORY
Berkley trade paperback edition / May 2001

The Penguin Putnam Inc. World Wide Web site address is
www.penguinputnam.com

Library of Congress Cataloging-in-Publication Data

Shapiro, Patricia Gottlieb.
Heart to heart : deepening women's friendships at midlife / Patricia Gottlieb
Shapiro.
p. cm.
Includes bibliographical references and index.
ISBN 0-425-17657-6
1. Middle-aged women—Psychology. 2. Female friendship. I. Title.

HQ1059.4 .S45 2001
305.244—dc21   00-066707

PRINTED IN THE UNITED STATES OF AMERICA

10 9 8 7 6 5 4 3 2 1

For my inner circle of friends

Contents

Acknowledgments

I want to thank my close friends first of all, because without them, I would have no reason to write this book. Norma Bolden, Jane Brooks, Anne Cogen, Diane Lachman, and Paula Slomsky have been a steady source of support and encouragement while I was working on this book and throughout the years.

Trying to understand my evolving and deepening connections with my friends led me to this project and to the fifty women who composed my research. I am grateful for the time each woman gave me and for the openness and honesty with which she shared her thoughts, feelings, and experiences. At the end of almost every interview I was offered names of other women to talk to. I also want to thank Barbara Goldberg, Talia DeLone, Martha Jablow, Barbara Myers, and Pecki Witonsky for their interview leads as well.

For their professional expertise and psychological insights, I owe a debt of appreciation to Jean Baker Miller, Harriet Lerner, and Paula Hardin. They gave freely of their time and knowledge. Susan Balis shared her wisdom in many conversations. She also read large sections of the manuscript. Her feedback raised important issues and helped clarify my thinking.

A number of other people read early drafts of selected chapters.

For their careful reading and insightful comments, I want to thank
Jane Brooks, Barbara DeLuca, Martha Jablow, and Dick Shapiro.
My agent, Carol Mann, made this book a reality. It has been a
pleasure to work with Lisa Considine, my editor at Berkley. She
was accessible, responsive, and showed a keen sensitivity to the
topic. Martha Jean Holubec made my life easier by transcribing
my tapes with accuracy and speed.

Many other friends, colleagues, and family members lent support as well. My sister, Anne Angerman, provided insights, edi-
torial feedback, and TLC. My sisters-in-law, Doris Feingold and
Lois Sykes, have also been there for me. My daughter Margot has
taken a keen interest in this project. Even over the long-distance
lines, her gentle caring came through. My son Andrew, too, has
been a big booster of me and my writing.

Lastly, I want to thank my best friend, my husband Dick, for
his abiding confidence in me, his encouragement in finding my
voice, and his loving presence in my life.

Introduction

Friends become more important to women at midlife, I told an audience of one hundred and fifty women when I gave the keynote address for a midlife women's conference at a hospital in Denver in 1997. What's more, I added, women often prefer the company of their friends to their husbands. Heads turned, women shifted uncomfortably in their seats, a buzz rippled through the audience. When I quoted Erica Jong, writing in her memoir about turning fifty—"Are men so interesting? To *themselves*, they are. Yet, lately, I find women far more interesting"—the audience roared.

They laughed because I said aloud what they all felt but had dared not acknowledge, even to themselves. Everyone in that audience knew instinctively that women *were* more interesting now, and that female friends mattered enormously.

Long after the lecture ended, that laughter-filled auditorium echoed in my ears. When I reflected on its meaning, I realized I had hit a nerve. Women had not fully recognized the growing importance of their friendships. Only when I contrasted their preference for female friends over the men in their lives did the message hit home.

While the laughter intrigued me professionally, it reassured me

personally. Friendships had become more central and more crucial to my life in the last ten years. When my mother died in 1988
(my father had died nine years earlier), I was forty-four. I had no
family in Philadelphia. Both of my husband Dick's parents died
within ten months of my mother. Andrew and Margot, our son
and daughter, then teenagers, were moving off in their own directions, as they should. My only sister lived two thousand miles
away. Although it sounds trite, my friends became my family and
supported me through my children's adolescence.

But it wasn't until Andrew and Margot left for college that I
turned to friends in a more life-sustaining way. Sure, I had more
time now and I enjoyed being with women, but I needed them
in a different way. I felt vulnerable and confused. With a huge
chunk of my life gouged out, I wasn't sure what remained of me.
Was I still a mother with the kids gone? Who was I now if I
wasn't mothering every day? As the roles and relationships I had
counted on for years shifted, they created a domino effect on the
rest of my life. Without kids at home, Dick and I had to renegotiate our relationship. My work, while engaging, did not fill the
void, as I had anticipated. An empty nest clearly meant I was
getting older. I could not deny that any longer.

Trying to make sense of these changes compelled me to connect
with other women. No longer did I insist on erecting a facade of
being "together." I *needed* to talk about my feelings and experiences. I *needed* confirmation from my friends that they had en-
countered similar disruptions. (They had, I learned.) I found that
the more I shared, the more my friends opened up. It seemed
easier to talk candidly, because by the time we had reached midlife, we had all had our hearts broken, whether through the death
of a loved one, a divorce, or angst over a child. None of us had
perfect lives and we didn't care if anyone else knew. With maturity

came acceptance. The shame that cloaked our vulnerabilities when we were younger had evaporated.

Not that my friendships were or are perfect. Far from it. I still struggle with the issue of expectations in a friendship. I wonder why an old friend continues to guard how much she reveals. I feel guilty over cutting ties with another longtime friend, as our lives take divergent paths. Should I have stayed in the relationship for old time's sake or could I have, at the least, handled my exit more gracefully?

While these issues can crop up between women of any age, at midlife our friendships take on a new immediacy. We know that neither we nor our friends will live forever. Many of us have lost dear friends to breast cancer or other diseases. We recognize the preciousness of life and cherish each other more than we did at a younger age.

ALMOST A HUNDRED years ago, in 1905, life expectancy was 48.7 years.[1] If women were lucky enough to be alive at age fifty, they were content to sit out the rest of their days in a rocking chair on the front porch, playing with their grandchildren. No longer. Today we can expect to live until seventy-nine.[2] We enjoy better health, fuller lives, and more options. We're determined to squeeze every ounce of living into our days, each in our own way.

Consider the diversity and complexity of our lives now. Some of us are celebrating our children's college graduations, as others fly to China to adopt baby girls. We are wrestling over divorce papers, toasting twenty-fifth anniversaries, and bickering over prenups. We are litigating in courtrooms, opening our own businesses, and escaping to the country. We're downsizing to smaller residences, buying vacations homes, and purchasing our first houses. We are burying our husbands, coming out as lesbians, and becoming grandmothers and stepmothers.

Whatever shape our lives take, the milestone of approaching—and turning fifty—affects us all, as do the physical changes that accompany the half-century mark. How we cope with those changes, the degree to which we accept them and see them as challenges rather than stressors, will determine our approach to the second half of life.[3]

We must also recognize that we live in a culture that worships youth and beauty and views midlife women as medical maladies—concerned with hot flashes, osteoporosis, and estrogen replacement therapy—as well as candidates for antidepressants. While the women's movement offered an alternative, more positive image of the older woman as architect of her own life, it can be challenging to integrate feminist beliefs that value our maturity with the ageist and sexist influences bombarding us in movies and advertising.[4]

Yet the women I interviewed—none household names—told me they have never felt more vital. Yes, they must contend with hot flashes, night sweats, fatigue, memory lapses, and erratic sleep patterns as well as changes in their sex drive. These shifts challenge their days but in no way demolish them. Often harder to accept are the outward signs of aging: the broadening hips, gray hair, crow's-feet, and double chins that greet us in the morning mirror.

Besides adjusting to physical changes, we must contend with the emotional repercussions of our shifting family roles and relationships. We witness our parents aging, growing frail, becoming ill. Many of us have become caregivers—both physically and emotionally—for our elderly mothers and fathers. We're exhausted from running. If they live nearby, we dash over before work to make sure they've taken their medications, rush to the supermarket to pick up a quart of milk, or cancel a meeting to take them to a doctor's appointment. When they live in another part of the country, we rack up enormous telephone bills "just checking in." And of course, the worry and concern, along with the guilt that we don't live closer, plagues us as we go about our lives.

More and more of us have buried our parents and must cope with the aftereffects of their deaths. Not only are we no longer anyone's child, but we have become the older generation. A frightening prospect on many levels. The blanket of protection our parents offered, the way their generation separated us from death, has evaporated. We now reign as matriarchs, sitting at the head of the table, wielding power in the family.

Launching our children also reminds us that we are becoming the older generation. Unless we gave birth late in life, our sons and daughters are moving out or have already left home. Letting go can be wrenching—or not, depending on the other stressors in our lives, the nature of our relationships with our children, and our feelings about our mothering. One woman told me she felt as though her arm had been amputated when her only daughter left home. Another felt "drunk with freedom." Scores of others fall somewhere in between those two extremes.

Once we come to terms with the loss, we face an uncharted stage of development—what author Gail Sheehy has called a "second adulthood." Without responsibilities for children, we are free to develop hobbies long forgotten, rediscover childhood interests, push our intellectual limits, pursue social or political agendas, and unearth pleasures buried years ago.

For women who never had children, whether by choice or by circumstance, the onset of menopause can bring a finality to that decision. Although a resurgence of regrets may occur at midlife, hopefully, healing has occurred by now.

With the winnowing of our family relationships, we have more leisure, even though most of us work full-time. By midlife, we've had a variety of work experiences, depending on when we entered the workforce, whether and when we had children, whether we received our education early or late in life, and whether divorce or widowhood affected our financial situation. While these experiences determine some of our attitudes toward work today, our priorities often shift as we get older. As we become more mindful of our mortality, we recognize that every day counts, so how we spend our time matters, whether we work for a salary or as a volunteer. Many of us now question whether financial reward can truly compensate for exhaustion and stress, and the price we continue to pay for driving ourselves to succeed.

Some find the thrill of achievement diminishes as they age. Others feel as though they are just beginning to come into their own as professionals. It often takes until midlife for women to gain the competence and confidence to become a leader or mentor in their field or to find their "voice" in the creative arts. Some late-bloomers decide to nurture a new "baby" in their fifties—a business, cause, or project they feel passionate about.[5]

AS WE TRY to understand and cope with the kaleidoscope of changes affecting us at midlife, it is our friends who provide stability and comfort. We feel less alone and less abandoned knowing they live around the corner or are only a phone call away. Just having someone listen to us and accept us without judgment reassures us. "We are so forgiving of one another and we need that," one woman commented. "The world is harsh. Our families are not where we want them. Friends are the people you can count on. I have two or three friends who check in every day."

But we don't wish simply to surround ourselves with lots of

casual acquaintances. We want meaningful connections. Our time is too valuable to waste on people we don't care about. We yearn to be with people we enjoy, talking about things that matter. And we want to have fun, whether we're browsing in a bookstore, singing in karaoke clubs, or fast-walking together.

"Until my early forties I really did have a sense that life was forever and I could put my entire universe into my work and there would always be more time later," a fifty-one-year-old writer with a fourteen-year-old daughter told me. "Now I realize there's less time and that these relationships are important to me. I don't have a lot of time for just chitchat friends and hanging around talking about clothes. I choose people I trust and who I can be honest with and who are empathic and fun. That's a new aspect of my life that's wonderful and still emerging. All I need to do is make it a priority. It's more meaningful than I ever knew it could be when I was, say, in my thirties."

At midlife women bring a confidence and maturity to their relationships that they didn't possess at thirty or even at forty. "I'm not as needy. I'm able to separate from my friends and not look to them to define myself," said a fiftyish woman who has been married twice. "It's a paradox: When I was younger I wanted to be someone's friend because she was cool or beautiful. I needed her approval for my own self-esteem. As I'm more aware of who I am and comfortable with that, I can separate and don't need *her* to validate *me*. I can appreciate her for who she is—but not as a mirror for myself."

Several studies support women's growing confidence at midlife. Ravenna Helson, Ph.D., director of the Institute of Personality Assessment and Research at the University of California/Berkeley, followed 101 graduates of Mills College from the age of twenty-two until they reached fifty-two. In young adulthood, these educated women were more "dependent, insecure and self-critical" than their husbands, but once they reached fifty, the women became confident, while their husbands grew more dependent and uncertain about their futures. David Gutmann, a psychologist who studied midlife psychological changes in the mid-eighties, attributed women's blossoming to giving up the parenting role, but more recent research doesn't support this view.[6] In the Mills College study, women's competence and self-confidence increased regardless of whether they had children. And regardless of their job status.[7]

At midlife we value our strengths and know our challenges. We've gained an acceptance of ourselves and others. We're not afraid to admit what we don't know. Even at this age, women told me they are still discovering what it means to be a true friend and yearn to learn more about how to enhance their connections with each other.

WE TAKE OUR friendships seriously, yet they have not always been regarded so. Few historians in the nineteenth century thought much about female friendships and virtually no one wrote about them. Yet letters and diaries of women who lived from the late 1890s through the mid-1900s show that women routinely formed emotional ties with each other—not only sisters and adolescent girls but mature women as well.[8] Until the mid-1970s, however, women's friendship attracted little attention. During the heyday of Freud's influence, from the 1940s to the 1960s, interest and research on the psychology of friendship came to a complete standstill.[9]

Historians, anthropologists, sociologists, and psychologists either ignored women's friendships, or belittled or trivialized them.[10] They saw them as "watery imitations of male camaraderie," shallow, and short-lived due to female jealousy.[11] Of course, these proclamations came from men, whose work revolved around the study of other men. In his seminal book on the adult male life cycle, psychologist Daniel Levinson emphasized men's relationship to society and minimized their attachment to others.[12] How contrary to women's experience: We grow *through* our connections. Levinson also observed that for men, friendship—with men or women—was "noticeable by its absence."[13] For that very reason, I have chosen not to focus on men's friendships at midlife.

Because of these sexist and historical biases, academic interest in women's friendships did not emerge until the women's movement of the 1960s and 1970s, as concern grew with all aspects of women's lives. Even then, however, feminists paid more attention to issues related to work and power (male concerns) than to relationships. In addition, women had to battle a culture that placed their relationships with their husbands and children on center stage and pushed their friendships backstage. They moved front and center only when the lead actors had other plans. This, despite studies that showed that the overwhelming majority of both married and single women had their deepest emotional relationship with a woman.[14]

"Many women have been good friends to each other all along. But they really weren't valued. The women's movement did change that. Before, women's friendships were almost sort of trivialized: 'Oh, that's a coffee klatch,' and it's just 'those girls' that talk all the time, that sort of thing. People didn't really credit the depth of it. In a funny way, I don't think women themselves even did," recalls Jean Baker Miller, clinical professor of psychiatry at Boston University Medical School and director of the Jean Baker Miller Training Institute at the Stone Center at Wellesley College.

The Stone Center is renowned for its comprehensive research program and its innovative theoretical work on women's psychological development. Jean Baker Miller and her colleagues were among the first to document the significance of relationships in women's lives. Their research challenged traditional male studies that contended that adults develop by separating from others. This groundbreaking work on the importance of connection for women's development provided the theoretical framework for this book.

When Jean Baker Miller was raising her children in the 1950s, she would meet her friends in the park and they'd chat as they watched their youngsters. Toward the end of the day, somebody would say, "Oh, it's five-thirty. I have to get home," she recalls. "Everybody understood that. You had to go take care of your husband's meal—that was the important thing. We just were sort of wasting time here, killing time till 'the real thing' happened. That wasn't so. Those women really mattered a lot, but we could never say it."

THIS IS THE first book to explore why friends matter at midlife, the special nature of the bond, and its roots and challenges. The book begins by putting friendship in perspective as a significant piece of women's development. We'll look at how the nature of friendship evolves as we age and what it means to us today. We'll also analyze the unique qualities of the midlife bond: how we support and challenge each other and how the sense of history affects longtime relationships. We'll see how the nature of our confiding deepens as women reveal in their own words the kinds of personal concerns they share with each other.

Next, we'll explore the impact of our early female role models to help us better understand the roots of our alliances today. We'll review the verbal and nonverbal messages we receive from our mothers and see their influence in forming and sustaining friend-ships. We'll also try to untangle the impact of our sisters to un-derstand how our early experiences with expectations, closeness, and competition affect us today.

As we spend more time together and our relationships deepen, negative feelings can emerge. Yet how difficult it is to acknowl-edge jealousy, anger, and competition! We'll learn from women who have mastered the art of constructive confrontation how this skill can boost our self-esteem and strengthen ties with friends.

The book will also explore the complicated relationship be-tween marriage and friendship. Most married women have expe-rienced a husband's resentment and jealousy over the time and energy they give to friends. But few of us recognize the hidden benefit of friendship: how it can complement and stabilize a mar-riage. For single women, friendships offer strength, support, and security. We'll examine the special meaning of friends to divorced, widowed, and never-married women.

As we age, we must inevitably face losing a friend to sickness or death. We'll explore how disease affects the connection, who remains a friend and who leaves, and the ways in which women support each other through crises. We'll hear from women on both sides of illness as we examine its ramifications on friendship.

Even though our first friendships date back to preschool, most of us are not experts in handling the thorny areas. We say we desire deep, lasting friendships. But even at our age, we don't always have the skills to make this happen. We're not quite sure what to say, so we don't tell a friend how much she means to us. We withdraw rather than handling hurts and disappointments openly. We hold back from reaching out to someone new because, we tell ourselves, she already has her friends. In reality, we're either uncertain about how to approach her or afraid of being rejected. Through suggested dialogues and guidelines, the book will help us develop the skills needed to strengthen connections, exit friendships with poise, and broaden our circle of friends.

The book will end with a discussion on befriending ourselves. Many of us are generous caregivers and nurturers but have difficulty carving out time to meet our own needs. We'll learn ways to balance our lives and replenish ourselves so we have more to give to all our relationships.

RELATIONSHIPS AND WOMEN'S issues have interested me ever since I received my education and training as a clinical social worker thirty years ago. My previous books dealt with women and their mentors, parenting a depressed child or adolescent, and women's growth and development after their children leave home. When I interviewed women about the way their lives changed once they launched their children, many talked spontaneously about how friends became more integrated in their lives, more important to them, and more fun. Those interviews provided the kernel of the idea for this book.

In writing *Heart to Heart* I had a dual purpose. I wanted to better understand my own friendships as well as explore the importance and meaning of friendship among my contemporaries, women at midlife. To do such an in-depth exploration, I felt I needed to hear from a wide range of women. I used the snowball method of sampling. I started with a small group of women I knew, who recommended others. I interviewed many of those women and usually left our meeting with the names of two or three others to call. The whole process snowballed until I had interviewed fifty women from all parts of the country—from big cities and small towns, rural regions and large metropolitan areas.

My sample consisted of twenty-nine married women and

twenty-one who were divorced, widowed, or never married. They ranged in age from forty-five to sixty years old. Ninety percent of my sample were Caucasians; 10 percent, African-Americans; one woman, a Puerto Rican. These women came from assorted religious backgrounds. Ten percent of my sample were homemakers; everyone else was employed. Their occupations included psychologists, business owners, teachers, interior decorators, marketing executives, writers, consultants, musicians, and human resource managers. All the women came from middle-class and upper-middle-class backgrounds.

I did not include lesbians in this study. After doing preliminary research on their friendships, a number of issues unique to lesbians emerged and I felt that I could not cover them adequately and thoroughly in this book.

I asked each woman to fill out a preliminary survey before our interview. The survey provided basic demographic data (age, religion, education, occupation, marital status, etc.) as well as preliminary information on their friendships. I learned how many women they confided in, whether their friends lived nearby or out of town, how their friendships had changed as they aged, and areas of concern to them. The knowledge gleaned from the survey allowed me to approach each woman with a better sense of her background and suggested a direction for the interview. I tape-recorded the interviews, which lasted from one to two hours. The tapes were then transcribed. I did follow-up interviews when I needed more information on certain points or further explanation.

Only one woman refused to speak to me; she said she didn't have time. Everyone else welcomed the opportunity to talk. Most told me they spent days ruminating on their friendships in preparation for our meeting. Although every woman I interviewed had thought about the meaning and nature of her friendships, many had not verbalized those thoughts. Some cried when speaking of a troubled relationship with a mother or the death of a friend. They joked that the interview felt like therapy, told me they appreciated the insights they gained from talking. When the interview ended, *they* thanked me.

AS I WORKED on this book, reviewing transcripts, analyzing women's relationships, double-checking sources and studies, writing and rewriting certain passages, I constantly thought about my own friendships. It was impossible not to: I was living them as I researched and wrote this book. During one particularly difficult week, I brought one friend home from the hospital following surgery, learned from another that she had breast cancer, and heard from a third that she was leaving her husband. Naturally, those events had an impact on me and on this book.

You'll find aspects of my life and my relationships interwoven with the experiences of the fifty women I interviewed. Research studies and commentary from experts support our stories. Talking with other women, sharing similar satisfactions and challenges, has certainly validated my experiences. As our commitment to our friendships shows, we long for connection. Giving voice to women's emotions and experiences unites us and affirms all our lives. I hope these personal stories will touch you and encourage you to think about your life and your relationships so you continue to cherish your ties with other women and deepen your friendships as you age.

Author's Note

I have changed all the names of interviewees and their personal identifying information to protect their privacy. I've also given my friends fictitious names. I haven't altered the details of my experiences with them, although I have changed or omitted some information that might specifically identify them.

Chapter One

The Midlife Bond

"The best mirror is an old friend."

Proverb

"Come Celebrate Beth's Big Birthday," the invitation beckoned. A computer-generated replica of my friend's five-year-old mug beamed on the cover. Inside, the details of a fiftieth birthday party: a luncheon for women only. At a small, elegant restaurant in center-city Philadelphia, twenty-five of us ranging in age from twenty-six to eighty-two gathered in early September. We were Beth's friends from work, school, the neighborhood, and her women's group as well as family members.

The luncheon started like any other, with small talk over the meal. Before dessert, one of her friends stood and invited everyone to participate in a ritual to commemorate Beth and her birthday. She passed out paper and pencils and asked that we take a few minutes to write a message for Beth on this important day. Then, pulling a large *challah,* a braided bread for ceremonial occasions, and a cup of honey from her bag, she explained the process. Everyone would stand, tear a piece of *challah,* dip it into the honey—a Jewish custom to ensure a sweet year—taste it, and then give her tribute.

One by one, each woman stood and spoke of Beth's warmth,

her insightfulness, her sensitivity, her generosity, her sense of humor. Tossing written notes aside, everyone spoke from the heart. A former neighbor, a friend of twenty-two years, choked back tears as she said, "You've been a sister to me." A new friend from work spoke of how happy she was to be included. Her mother told her how proud she felt. Some of us had written poems or "Top Ten" lists as part of our gifts, and read those. We howled at her lifelong quest for the perfect chicken salad sandwich, the addition of her name to AARP's mailing list. Because her friends came from so many different spheres of her life, many of us did not know each other, yet by the end of the afternoon, the room buzzed with energy and radiated with warmth. A few days after the party, Beth said to me, "That afternoon was a gift. It was simply nirvana. I felt so nurtured."

As a participant in Beth's celebration, I felt as though I had received a gift, too. No doubt, each woman there went home feeling good. Every one probably reflected on her special connection with Beth as well as her other friendships and what they meant to her. I know I did. I also thought about how typical this event was of women's friendships at midlife: It was warm, giving, honest, and open. Several other women have told me about similarly moving birthday celebrations. One, whose friends also honored her fiftieth with personal tributes, said, "These were things that would have been said at my funeral. But I could be there and hear them!"

Not only do we appreciate our friends at midlife, but we tell them how much they mean to us. To say that friendship matters now is an obvious and gross understatement. Every woman at midlife knows that. To understand *why* friendship has become such an important, integral part of our lives, we need to look at it within the context of women's development. Observing how our friendships ebbed and flowed through earlier life stages gives us a historical perspective on our alliances today. Understanding the nature of the bond itself validates our own ties.

As we experience physical and emotional upheavals, shifting family ties, and a reordering of our work priorities at midlife, it is our friends who keep us anchored and grounded amid the sea of changes within us and around us. A journalist told me, "I feel a tangible sense that my friends are there like rocks surrounding me: unchanging, encouraging, approving beings in my life." What a powerful image: Each woman stands at the center of her life, surrounded by a caring circle of friends—steady and solid as rocks. Together, these circles create a web of interlocking orbits. Each woman has enough space around her to grow, yet knows that her friends stand ready to protect her, to bolster her when she falters, to encourage her when she hesitates and cheer when she succeeds.

A Strong Base

From experiences of my own, like Beth's birthday luncheon, and the interviews with the fifty women who composed my research for this book, I've learned that women at midlife hunger for deep, intimate relationships with each other. They yearn to be candid and genuine with their friends. They want to feel they can be "real" and discuss whatever is on their minds and in their hearts.

As Chilean novelist Isabel Allende said, "After fifty most of the bullshit is gone. I don't have any time to waste. I don't have time for gossip or greed or revenge or undirected anger. I'm angry at very concrete things now and focus it into action. I know myself much better. I know my body and I know what becomes me and what doesn't. I don't make the mistake of wearing miniskirts, for example. I look terrible in pants and miniskirts. I know how to dress so that I feel more confident than I *ever* did before."[1]

Of course, confidence comes from within, not from wearing the right-length skirt. The self-assurance we develop as we age allows us to approach our friendships from a strong internal base. The neediness and desperation that strained our relationships when we were younger has diminished. Paula Hardin, author and director of Midlife Consulting Services in Chicago, comments, "As we evolve as a person and become more whole, our friendships are much more profound and deep. I don't find a friend out of looking for something to fill my empty places. I find them because they are just wonderful to be with. Our lives are better because we have one another."

When she was younger, she says she would accept situations in friendships that she won't tolerate anymore. "I would put up with not being real because maybe I wasn't quite real myself all the time. But now I won't do that," she says. In the past, she would let herself be used. She would try to "rescue" friends who had enormous problems and then would become frustrated because they didn't follow her excellent advice. That changed, she believes, as she became more mature and understood how her need to fix other people's problems stemmed from feeling responsible at a young age for a chronically ill mother. As she allowed others to learn from the natural consequences of their choices, she was able to give up control and simply be supportive. In turn, she stopped relying on others to make her happy and took responsibility for herself.

According to an unpublished doctoral dissertation by Sophie Jacobs Bronstein, women reported an increased sense of security and self-worth as the major impact of friendship on their lives. Being supported gave them more poise, a better sense of self, and enabled them to make things happen for themselves in a positive way.[2] My own research revealed similar findings. When I asked my interviewees how their friendships changed them, I received fifty different answers, but I could summarize them in four basic responses: "When I felt unlovable, my friends gave me unconditional love." "They gave me self-acceptance." "They made me warmer and more giving." "They believed in me."

Psychiatrist Jean Baker Miller, author of the classic *Toward a New Psychology of Women* and director of the Jean Baker Miller Training Institute at Stone Center at Wellesley College, credits relationships with giving women an inner sense of certainty at midlife. "What really makes a difference for women is that underneath it all, women have been involved more closely in relationships and grown from that," she notes. "Whereas men may have *done* things, they haven't been as closely involved in the give-and-take of relationships. That leaves them more with that kind of hollowness that can happen at mid-life to men. Relationships make a difference, a big difference."

The very nature of a treasured friendship instills confidence in women, because they feel valued and supported. At the same time, we come to midlife more assured, thanks to four or five decades of living. After all, we've been involved in friendships as far back as we can remember.

A Long History

Black-and-white snapshots cram my childhood photo album. My mother and father and my grandparents pose in dozens of ways with little Patti: propping me on their hips, holding my hand on the street corner, sitting with me on the sofa, and after age four, squeezing my little sister into the shot. One nonfamily member stands out in my album: my best friend Jan. From our silly smiles, you can tell we love posing—in the snow in our winter coats and hats, in the spring in jeans, flannel shirts, and saddle shoes, on Halloween in our mothers' dresses. In every photo, we're holding hands.

Jan and I grew up in similar circumstances. We both came from middle-class families and had businessmen as fathers. But her mother worked in the family leather-goods store (my mother didn't work outside the home). Lizzie Mae, a big, warm African-American woman, cooked, cleaned the house, and cared for Jan and her sisters while their parents worked. We didn't have household help. I remember walking into Jan's house after school and smelling eggplant simmering on the stove. It seemed so exotic to me. My mother never made eggplant. I learned then that everyone doesn't do things the way we did in our little brick house on Wolf Street in Racine, Wisconsin.

Through our grade-school pals, we learn that we're not only members of a family but part of a peer group as well. We get our first lessons in inclusion and exclusion, companionship and kindness, as well as in cruelty and neglect from our elementary-school buddies.[3] Much has been written about how boys and girls play differently: how boys, through team sports, learn how to cooperate and compete, while girls, who usually play in pairs, value connecting and confiding. No matter how they play in the school yard, though, home remains the hub of a youngster's existence.

In adolescence, that changes dramatically. Friends become supremely important as teens struggle for their independence and attempt to forge their own identities. Classic Freudian theory pitted teenage girls against their mothers, stressing that they must separate to form their own identity. Recent feminist theory, particularly research from the Stone Center at Wellesley College, has challenged that notion, asserting that young girls do not want or need to sever the bond with their mothers. Instead, mother and daughter stay connected—only they renegotiate the tie so the mother recognizes and respects how her daughter is changing and developing into her own person. This perspective represents a more accurate portrayal of women's experience. As we'll see throughout this book, women grow through connection. "Intimacy goes along with identity, as the female comes to know herself . . . through her relationships with others," psychologist Carol Gilligan explains in her landmark book, *In a Different Voice*.[4] Men, on the other hand, separate these two tasks. For them, identity precedes intimacy.

When we were in our twenties, friendships often took a backseat to building careers and forming romantic attachments.[5] As we raised our families, we gravitated to women with children the same ages as ours. Some of us formed long-standing friendships in those early child-raising years. We offered each other support as we contended with toilet training, sibling rivalry, Little League schedules, first crushes and first periods, and drugs and dating. Women who had best friends checked in with each other almost daily, but many of us didn't share real intimacies with each other during these years.

For one thing, we were more competitive in those days, especially concerning our children. How could you share your innermost fears about your child or doubts about yourself as a parent if you had to appear as "the good mother" to the outside world? Secondly, our husbands often felt jealous when we shared our precious free time with other women rather than with them. Between work, family, home, and community commitments, nurturing friendships felt like a luxury we couldn't afford—unless we had become died-in-the-wool feminists in college. Feminists, according to Denver psychotherapist Anne Angerman, MSW, always valued their women friends, made them a top priority on a par with their husbands, and were open and frank from day one.

For women who went through a divorce while raising their children, that crisis often deepened friendships, especially with other divorcees. Without a spouse, friends became a lifeline: to commiserate with, to give support, and to just have fun with. Then, as we all move through our forties—whether we have teenagers at home, children already launched, or are single women who never became mothers—friendships matter again.

Tighter Ties

Several studies have suggested that by the time women reach their forties and fifties, their networks become smaller but they interact with their friends more frequently and the content of their friendships becomes more specialized.[6] British scholar Terri Apter, who interviewed eighty women between the ages of forty and fifty-three for her book *Secret Paths: Women in the New Midlife,* found that these women made nearly as many references to friendship as did teenage girls. Women told her their friendships were as much fun as they had been during adolescence but were more fluid: Cliques no longer ruled their existence but "whole rivers" of friends streamed into their lives.[7]

Apter also discovered that the women in her sample felt freer from concern about how other women judged them and they expected them to evaluate them more leniently and more favorably. Unlike adolescents, who hide their areas of vulnerability from friends, midlife women talked openly of their insecurities, free of shame.[8] My interviewees also reported that their friendships had reached a deeper level of honesty at midlife and that they now shared intimacies freely without fear of being criticized.

"I now really have friendships whereas before I probably had loose associations. So my friendships are very rich. They have lasted throughout each of our personal crises, through whatever happens in the world. We live in the same city, we live apart— we still remain intact," a fiftyish single woman told me. "The quality of intimacy is what now really qualifies friendships for me. We can just be drop-dead honest and there's no judgment and no crap going on. You just feel safe, honored, respected, like family."

Why are we neither judged nor judgmental? By the time we reach midlife, few of us have escaped the random hand of fate. We've either survived a divorce, a death, or a physical or emotional setback in ourselves or our family. Humbling and leveling, these experiences remind us of how little we know and how many of our earlier judgments stemmed from our own insecurity. Now, feeling more confident and comfortable with ourselves, we've become more accepting of ourselves and our friends.

"I see much more tolerance, acceptance of one another and of a broader range of behaviors and emotions as we get older," a therapist told me. This broad blanket of acceptance influences our friendships on so many levels. We're no longer super-sensitive to petty slights. The competition over kids and careers has almost vanished. We still feel envious and jealous from time to time, as we'll see in Chapter 4, but we better understand the issues that create these emotions. Our expectations are more realistic. We know how to truly "be there" for each other.

More Than a Shoulder to Cry On

Commiseration, say psychotherapists and best friends Luise Eichenbaum and Susie Orbach, "is the capacity to show that one understands what another might be feeling and comforting her or him, often by producing instances in which one has been similarly made to feel hurt/angry/irritated/betrayed."⁹ We all know how reassuring this kind of support can be—when we experience our first hot flash, when we lose our jobs, when we discover a lump in one of our breasts, or when our kids leave for college.

Dana, forty-nine, recalls her friends' support a couple of years ago when Jillian, her fourteen-year-old daughter, started pulling away from the family. For years Dana, who runs a consulting business from her home, would arrange her day so she'd be available when Jillian came home from school at three-thirty. But suddenly Jillian wanted no part of her mother. She spent nearly all her time in her room with the door closed. She'd surface for dinner then, after fifteen minutes, ask, "Can I be excused?" and return to her lair. She wasn't rude, just distant. She also stopped confiding in Dana or initiating any conversation.

"My friends said how sorry they were and how painful it was. That was enormously comforting. I needed someone to mirror back that this was a big deal. It's hard for Jim to listen." Her husband either dismisses the problem and encourages her to forget it or suggests solutions. Her friends, on the other hand, offer compassion and a sense that she is not alone.

When we commiserate, we're not just "having a good moan together," say Eichenbaum and Orbach. Rather, there's an implicit demand to see the situation as it is presented and not to question the other person's perception.¹⁰ Dana's friends listened, then shared how their sons and daughters had separated and how painful it was. They also told her when and how they had returned to the family fold. In one conversation her good friend Rosellen told Dana how her daughter at thirteen began to angrily refute everything she said and laughed at her for being so square. Rosellen was devastated. "But it was very reassuring for me," Dana says, "because I know this family well and today I see this young woman at age nineteen who's incredibly positive, respectful, and affectionate. This helped me see it as a phase."

Rosellen reassured Dana, "Jillian will come back. You've laid the groundwork for a strong, trusting relationship—those are the ones who come back." Dana said that those encouraging words helped her hang in and not react in some very "unparental, guilt-inducing way" toward Jillian.

As we get older, we feel comfortable distancing ourselves from a friend so we can help her move ahead. No longer dependent on another's approval for our self-esteem, we're able to challenge her without worrying that we'll lose her affection. After we commiserate, we then try to help extricate her from her problem by presenting a differing point of view, provoking her to look at her reaction, or challenging her to change the status quo.

Dana's friends told her she didn't have to suffer passively on the sidelines waiting for Jillian to grow up. They suggested she refocus her energies toward friends, other activities, and Jim—anything besides mothering. They also urged her and Jim to take the trip to London they had dreamed of for years (and they did).

Role Modeling

When we offer our friends the kind of support Dana received, we can serve as role models for each other. How often have you been in a pinch and wondered what a good friend would do in a similar circumstance? I often think of a former therapist of mine who framed every relationship issue with two questions: "What do you owe and what do you deserve?" Balancing the answers to those questions helps me sort out the problem at hand. Dana's friend often asks, "Well, have you thought about this?" or "What do *you* want to do?" Then she may offer, "This is what *I'd* do."

Sometimes we live vicariously through friends who are role models. What they do seems beyond our grasp: the pal who climbs mountains while we're afraid of heights or the chum who thrives on lecturing while we hesitate to speak up in an adult-night-school class. While these friends *seem* so different from ourselves, I don't believe they are. Nor is it a coincidence that we choose them. These women attract us because they speak to a piece of us that has been hidden or undeveloped.[11] I have a new friend, for example, who expresses her feelings so effortlessly and fluently—something I wish came more easily for me. I admire this quality and secretly hope that if I associate with her, either some of her skill will rub off on me or her ease of expression will free me up to do the same.

Such role-model friends challenge us to take risks and move beyond commiseration. That can be frightening, but knowing we have the steady support of a friend enables us to push ahead *despite the fear* and do things that would be formidable alone. The relationship itself empowers us.[12] This occurred on a grand scale in the 1996 movie *First Wives' Club.* College friends Goldie Hawn, Bette Midler, and Diane Keaton reconnect some twenty years later after the funeral of a mutual friend who committed suicide. All in their late forties and married to wealthy men, they realize when they sit down to lunch that they gave their husbands the best years of their lives. Now they've learned that each of their husbands is having an affair with a younger woman.

They spend hours sharing their individual stories—their hurt, anger, and betrayal—and lamenting their situation. But after a while one of them asks, "What do we want?" Not simply revenge, they agree. They want justice. Each woman, emboldened and empowered by the other two, stands up to her husband and forces him to write a check to finance their new venture. The movie ends with the trio triumphantly opening a crisis center for troubled and abused women.

A Seasoned Perspective

In the course of my interviews I met many women who had been friends with one another for more than twenty years. I, too, have known most of my own closest friends for almost two decades. I met them through the neighborhood, through my children's play groups and schools, through my interests in tennis and writing, and through other friends. Like all long-lived friendships, mine have weathered crises with kids, illnesses, relationship difficulties, and deaths. We've also celebrated plenty of good times together.

These enduring friendships generate a sense of history and memory, which creates an indelible bond. We don't often realize at the time that simply "being there" cements the connection. Take Sandi, a teacher, who has been best friends with Kim, another teacher, for twenty-four-years. Sandi remembered the exact incident that tightened their tie: Sandi's two-year-old daughter had a serious accident and had to be rushed to the hospital. Sandi recalls, "Kim was there. That's what did it. She was just there." In the hospital. When Sandi's daughter came home. While she was recovering. Six weeks later the tables were turned: When Kim's mother died, Sandi was there for her every day.

I heard many other poignant stories of how a crisis—a divorce, a husband's coming out, death of a parent, illness of a child—deepened a friendship. One woman, however, described a different kind of juncture. Ruth, a pediatrician from Denver, told me that she had a serious argument in the early stages of every single friendship, as if she and her friend needed to determine the ground rules for being honest with each other. "That argument established the friendship and provided some sort of a bottom-line understanding that we were serious about it," she recalls. When her friend Meredith gave birth to her daughter six years before Ruth became pregnant, Ruth was very jealous. "I was so upset. I felt as if I was losing my friend," she says. "I didn't know how to deal with it and I was probably inappropriate. I was making all sorts of demands on her, because I felt excluded."

It took Ruth a long time to resolve her feelings. The two women talked about the situation for months. Meredith didn't like the side of Ruth that emerged, but felt committed to the relationship and persevered until Ruth could accept that Meredith could indeed be a mother *and* a loyal friend.

For most other women, myself included, longtime friendships have evolved slowly and deepened gradually as trust grew from sharing increasingly private confidences and vulnerabilities. Being present in each other's lives over a span of ten, twenty, or thirty years gives us a unique perspective. "We have memories for each other. We remember history," one woman told me. "When you're young, you're busy watching life develop. When you're older, you have to use wisdom and memory in order to honestly help a friend."

But we do more than simply remember. We witness one another's lives and affirm them. "A witness validates just by knowing," another explained. "A spouse or children can't do it in the same way. Our parents can't—most of them are sick or dying. Our friends become our walking histories."

Not only do we remember and bear witness, but we accept each other. By now we know each other's shortcomings and idiosyncrasies. But we hang in anyway. When my friend Sara obsesses about a minor decision in her life, such as which hotel to stay at for a business trip to Boston, I listen and offer the pros and cons. I know she'll work it out, but she needs to cover all the bases, again and again. (I understand, because I have a similar tendency to obsess.) When I pick up Jackie for dinner or the movies, I know she won't be ready. It used to bother me that she was always late, but now I know: That's just who she is; she leads a hectic life.

Because our friends have known us so long and so well, they can help us put our current concerns into a larger perspective and examine whether our present modus operandi jibes with our values, our past decisions and choices, and our sense of self. For Christine, fifty-five and the director of a social service agency in Minneapolis, her best friend of thirty years, Darlene, provides this type of sounding board. Christine left the convent five years ago, after spending almost twenty-five years in the order. Darlene, a social worker who lives in Boston, remains in the convent.

Their weekly long-distance phone calls have changed in the last few years, Christine notes. They still report what happened and talk about what they do, but she says, "There's a greater sense of sharing the impact it has on us and on the texture of our lives. It's not just the feeling component. It's putting it in a larger perspective of how it affects today and also the future. Instead of looking at our lives in terms of pieces and events, we're sharing more about what this particular piece means in the whole of our lives."

As a social worker, Christine always valued her listening skills, but as a newly appointed director of an agency, she has been forced to become more assertive, even aggressive. Their programs need a massive infusion of funds, so Christine must persuasively present the agency's needs to community leaders. "I'm no longer only a listener," she says. "This arena is causing me to be a fighter, which isn't the way I know myself."

Christine is now exploring—with Darlene's help—whether she

feels comfortable developing that side of her personality. "How much of that is good and how much of that destroys the me that I've come to appreciate?" Christine wonders. Like many midlife women, Christine and Darlene talk on a different level than they did at thirty or even forty, when they were still forming their identities. Christine knows who she is but wants to continue growing. She can try to broaden her identity as helper/listener to incorporate "fighter," which would be a challenge for her. She is also free to reject the new label, but that may mean the loss of her new position. With Darlene's guidance, Christine will reach a decision that feels right for her.

"A Sacred Trust"

I am sitting across the table from a good friend. I listen as she talks, gesturing, laughing, scowling, her voice rising. The coffee gets cold as she describes an encounter with a boss, a confrontation with a child, her partner's remark, a new insight into herself. She leans closer, lowers her voice, shares a confidence. Sometimes she simply rolls her eyes; no more need be said. With words spoken and unspoken she tells me, "This is how I feel," "This is what I'm experiencing," "This is what bothers me."

At some point in the conversation, ever so subtly, we shift roles. This time my friend listens—eyes focused, head nodding, attention riveted—while I speak.

We've all participated in this scene hundreds of times. Over bagels and coffee, salads and iced tea, or pasta and wine, we connect with our friends. Sometimes seeking advice, sometimes just wanting to be heard, always sharing bits and pieces, or whole cloths, of our lives. Close friendships among women rest on such "shared intimacies, self-revelation, nurturance and support" while men's relationships with each other tend to focus on shared activities, usually watching or playing sports. Their talk usually centers on work, sports, and advising each other on investing, home repairs, or cars.

Women reserve such moments of connection for a few select friends. Among my sample, 64 percent confide in four to six women, with their friends equally split between those living in the same town and those in other parts of the country. The remainder of my sample had one to three confidantes; more than half of those lived nearby. Only one woman admitted to having no close friends. Of course, we all have neighbors, colleagues at work, and other acquaintances. But this book focuses on our relationships with our closest friends.

What do we actually divulge to each other? If you have such confidantes, the substance of these discussions will come as no surprise to you. But if you think your conversations and your friendships lack a certain depth or intimacy, these illustrations will show you what you're missing. Such openness and emotional sharing require "a sacred trust," which is how one woman described her bond with her best friend.

In response to the question "What do you talk to your friends about?" I heard the following:

From a fifty-one-year-old homemaker with two children in their late twenties: "We talk about everything. Really. We talk about our relationship with our children, our concern about our relationships with God, our jobs, the different people we encounter in our jobs and how we relate to them, our spouses if we have concerns about them. Decorating and home crafts, current events."

From a fifty-four-year-old married woman with four grown daughters: "I have a couple of friends whose parents are aging, and illness is as much in their lives as my own. That's a window of opportunity to talk about our own aging. What will we do when we get old? How do we feel about our mortality? The conversation starts on the practical level but tends to go a lot deeper."

She goes on. "We talk about spiritual issues: How do you keep yourself growing? How do you stay open? That's another question that I could come at in a million ways. It's not 'Where are you traveling?' but 'How do you stay alive or lively?' 'What are you reading and what are you getting out of it?' My questions are about how we live and why we are living, so these can reverberate through movies, books, or travels."

From a forty-nine-year-old widow with a teenage son: "I'll talk about my fear of death, problems with my son, stuff that goes on in my life, men I meet. But some things I don't discuss with anybody. Like certain terrors about things that are going on with me. I just keep that for my journal.

"When we were younger, talking about your sex life was a big deal," she continues. "That's not really important now at all. So that's one thing that we don't talk about. If I'm having an affair, I might talk about it, but I won't talk about sex except in kind of a funny way. We talk about money, our children, our homes, our feelings about life, mistakes we've made, reflections upon our parents' lives . . ."

Indeed. We cover the gamut, from the minutiae of the day (the great buy we got on a lined raincoat) to life-and-death issues. But how deep do we really go with our closest friends? The following situation illustrates the kind of meaty, personal concerns that women share with each other at midlife. **Kathryn**, a fifty-one-year-old painter married for twenty-five years to an executive with two grown sons from a previous marriage, has never had children of her own. Two years ago, when her husband Mac took early retirement, they moved from Hartford to La Jolla, California. Around the same time a boating accident killed her fifteen-year-old nephew. Although Kathryn had a group of friends back east whom she considered close, she had never tapped into them before.

Kathryn took the move very hard. For the first time in her life she started sharing her anger and discontent with her Hartford friends in lengthy long-distance calls. "No more happy talk," she told me. "I really got down to the nut of what was bothering me and sought help with that from my friends."

She vented her anger at her husband for retiring. "It was just totally weird," she recalls. "We had worked toward his early retirement for years. It's something that we both wanted, but adjusting to his physical presence was really difficult for me, and I think especially so because I am a painter, and do need that private space and time. All of a sudden I couldn't paint with him around. We have since worked it out, but the anger about his retirement, I really, really needed help with."

Her friends always listened, she said, particularly when she recounted conflicts with Mac. They pointed out, delicately, when they thought she was unfair or unreasonable and reminded her of how she had handled similar situations in the past. One friend suggested she rent a studio for herself. Another questioned her about her life in La Jolla, which, she said, "allowed me to hear myself speak about it and reinforce that, indeed, I did have a new life and I was negotiating this difficult transition."

Kathryn also tried to make sense of her young nephew's death. Talking about that, however, revived her own loss in not being able to have a child, which resulted in further anger at her husband. "That was really deep stuff for me, and I was feeling very isolated out here, not having anyone to talk to except Mac, and he was the very one I was mad at."

Kathryn had never before shared such private problems with friends. Perhaps the distance made it safer for her to reveal more

now. Long-distance friendships ensure a certain emotional security.[13] We can control the timing and length of the call and don't
have to worry about running into someone unexpectedly at the
supermarket or shopping mall. Without facial expressions or body
language that show approval or disapproval, it's easier to expose
our vulnerabilities, as many people have discovered when they
form relationships over the Internet.

As a result of that sharing, whether because of the safety of
distance or out of sheer need, Kathryn's friendships have deepened. Up until now, she considered herself self-sufficient and able
to handle problems on her own. She was not *unsatisfied* with her
earlier friendships; she just seemed to have few intimacy needs.
All of a sudden she could not guide herself alone; she needed a
helping hand.

Typically in a friendship pair (as in a marriage), one member
has a stronger desire for intimacy than the other. Yet, according
to an interesting study, both members can feel equally satisfied
with the relationship—unless the one with greater intimacy needs
feels hers aren't being met. In that case, the woman with fewer
needs would feel more content, because she expects less and gives
less, while her friend with higher expectations will feel disappointed and shortchanged.[14] Consider the relationship between
Sigi, who has five close friends, and Pam, who considers Sigi her
best and only friend. With several friends, Sigi has many opportunities for sharing and brings less neediness to each relationship,
while Pam anticipates that her friendship with Sigi will meet all
her emotional needs. Sigi cannot possibly give enough, so she will
undoubtably disappoint Pam.

Not only do we all have different intimacy needs but they
change as we mature and our relationships shift. In her younger
days, when Kathryn left a city, she said good-bye to all her friends.
But with this move, she says, "I really needed to feed those roots

that were established. As I've matured, I realized I need close female associations. When I was younger, I concentrated more on who I was, finding my niche in life, and establishing my relationship with my husband. But now those kinds of issues have been settled for the most part, so friendships are much more important. Being known is real important to me in middle age."

We all want to be known, yet for most of us, certain sensitive areas remain private, off-limits. Ruth, the pediatrician who described how an argument solidified each of her friendships, believes that a sacred space surrounds each of her friends. "There is an expression in Judaism: 'the fence around the Torah.' It means you protect certain principles so you keep them sanctified," she explains. "I want to be intimately involved with my friends and know about their lives, and they want to know about mine. At some point we had to understand where you could trespass and where you could not.

"Why would I need to have a fight with everybody?" she wonders. "Because if we're going to be so intimate, we cannot trespass into areas that are going to hurt. I protect the sanctity of my friends and my friendships by not violating that area. But I didn't know what that area was until I found that moment of argument. Once I have the argument, I don't need it anymore. I would never go in those areas again. Never. I don't need to. Because I really respect each person."

Although most of us cannot pinpoint a defining argument in each of our friendships, with time—often by trial and error—we, too, learn which areas are off-limits. We respect those limits and, like Ruth, do not trespass again.

A Patchwork Quilt

Many of us have friends who are just like us. They come from the same age group, the same race, religion, and social class. Yet in my interviews, I was also struck by the variety and diversity among midlife women's friends. Take Bobbi, a forty-nine-year-old divorced, lapsed Catholic who is an art dealer. Her closest friends are fifty, sixty, seventy, and ninety years old. They are Jewish, Quaker, and Catholic; married, divorced, and single. She met them through a seminar on world religions twenty years ago. What continues to draw them together? "We're all spiritual explorers," she said. Although the women rarely meet as a group anymore, it served as a springboard for Bobbi to meet like-minded women; then she developed lifelong friendships with each of them.

Many other women told me they, too, have diverse friends. They're not necessarily drawn together by a common theme, but have gathered slowly over the years, each one representing a different part of their lives. While these people may have been marginally present when our careers, marriages, and children were young, they come to the fore at midlife. Not only do we have more time for a variety of friends, but because we feel more secure within ourselves, we are better able to tolerate—or even welcome—differences. We're less influenced by convention, freer to follow our own interests and instincts, and care less what others think.

We become the hub of a wheel with our friends, many of whom hardly know each other, as spokes. They meet only when we draw them together for a special event, like my friend Beth's fiftieth birthday party. One woman told me, "Each of my friends represents a part of me that needs to be connected. They're my reading friends, my spiritual friends, my exercise friends, my just-have-fun friends. They represent the wide scope of myself. I'm able to tolerate that many relationships because I connect to that part of my own energy when I'm with them."

Carol, fifty-six, a bookstore owner recently widowed, indicated that her closest friend is a widow, too. She also has a large circle of freewheeling friends interested in Buddhism, shamanism, and alternative kinds of religion; a group of younger friends with toddlers as well as a seventy-year-old friend who shares her passion for nature photography. "I'm just drawn in very many ways, but I'm not part of a circle. I don't do well in situations like that," she says. "My friendships now, especially since my husband died, have provided a tremendous network. I almost feel like I'm floating on the caring that I'm getting from people."

Our Security Blankets

Diverse friends inject a welcome shot of adrenaline into our lives. At the same time, though, we still need our security blankets. As we cope with shifting relationships in our families, we need to know that some things *won't* change, that certain people will always be there. What better way to gain that sense of belonging than to reconnect with friends from childhood, high school, or college? One of my friends went to a spa with five high-school buddies to celebrate their fiftieth birthdays. Another began an annual retreat several years ago with six college friends, most of whom she hadn't spoken to in thirty years. I myself tracked down my roommate and best friend from college a few years ago. I had not seen her or spoken to her since we graduated in 1966.

Gerri and I met during our sophomore year of college after we both transferred to the University of Wisconsin. We roomed together, traveled abroad together. When we graduated, she set out for law school in Cambridge; I headed to Philadelphia for social-work school. The day we parted I told her that I wanted to keep in touch. She said she'd never forget me but warned, "I'm not a writer."

For the first several years I sent notes. No answer. After my children came, I sent photos. No reply. Eventually, I gave up trying to contact her. But each month when my alumni magazine arrived, I'd scan the news looking for word of her. Over the years I learned that she had moved to Texas, specialized in immigration law, married, and had a family. Several years ago, before a trip south, I tracked down her phone number and called her on what I thought was a whim. "Just tell me where to meet and I'll be there," she told me. Over bagels and coffee in an airport deli, we tried to reconstruct the last thirty years of our lives. Sitting across the table from her felt so familiar—we had eaten hundreds of meals together—and yet oddly strange. I would have recognized her anywhere but, I realized later, I didn't get her jokes.

These companions from another era help us recapture a part of our lives long gone. Who but Gerri remembers the Greek god I swooned over in Athens? How we hitchhiked through Europe in high heels and backpacks? Or how about the childhood friend who came over to watch *The Howdy Doody Show* every day after school? When you talk about your mother, she knows *exactly* what you mean. Keeping in touch with old pals gives us a sense of security, keeps those earlier years alive, and helps us remember our younger selves.

Several studies have shown that girls, between eight and eleven years old, radiate confidence, speak their minds, flaunt their smarts. But once they reach adolescence, they go underground, squelching their vitality in an attempt to conform to rigid cultural standards for women.[15] Psychologist Emily Hancock believes that buried within each adult woman lies "a distinct, vital self first articulated in childhood" that gets cut off in the process of growing up. Our task as women, says Hancock, is to reclaim the authentic identity we embodied as girls.[16] Our childhood friends, by recalling our youthful days, can help us become more authentic at midlife—if we can tap into and absorb aspects of our younger selves. Gerri reminds me of my free-spirited days before marriage and children, when I toured Europe without an itinerary or a reservation. I wish I had more of that spontaneity in my life today.

Of course, some women never lose touch with high-school or college friends. Think of the years and years of camaraderie and closeness shared by Vivi, Teensy, Caro, and Necie, the four Southern women in the best-selling novel *Divine Secrets of the Ya-Ya Sisterhood.* Such long-lasting friendships can be sustaining and enriching, as we discussed earlier. The danger is, however, that you can feel so secure in a close-knit group that you don't venture beyond this circle and make new friends, or that you send subtle signals to others that the group is closed and they're not welcome. A clique can be stifling and prevent you from growing.

Discriminating Taste

At midlife, we can afford to be more selective in our choice of friends. We don't need to be surrounded by a gang to feel good about ourselves, nor do we need the approval of a crowd to boost our esteem. A forty-nine-year-old human resource manager spoke for scores of women when she said, "I only spend time now with people I really care about. I'm really very selfish with my time."

Inevitably, part of that discrimination entails letting go of certain friends. Some we've outgrown. Others we've grown tired of: We know their script before they begin their litany. Some relationships just feel too "high maintenance." They sap us emotionally.

Rita had such a friend, a neighbor who seemed pleasant enough when they first met; then they started walking together two nights a week. "After a while all she did was complain. I would come home exhausted," Rita recalls. "It was horrible. I thought, oh my God, what have I done? But I had a very hard time telling her, and therefore I stopped walking. I didn't know how to be direct. I don't even know if I could today."

Fortunately for Rita, her job transferred her to another part of the country, so she had a legitimate reason to break off the friendship. Unfortunately, Rita's reluctance to assert herself and end a nonmutual friendship is all too common.

How difficult to part with someone, whether a new acquaintance or an old friend. Feelings of guilt, obligation, and—especially with old cronies—a sense of history nag us: Maybe we *should* save the alliance. Yet thinking of the sheer relief of escaping from another boring or toxic encounter overpowers the "shoulds." Only two of the women I interviewed actually discussed why they were ending an association with the friend with whom they were severing ties. All the others let friendships that weren't working wither away through neglect and indifference. They stopped returning phone calls, ignored offers to get together, or pleaded prior commitments.

Obligation does not create positive connections. It breeds resentment and anger. At midlife we want to pick and choose our voluntary associations for our own reasons. Many of us purposely let peripheral friendships die so we can focus on the relationships that have a potential for a deeper connection.

Author, biologist, and psychologist Joan Borysenko believes that when we eliminate those commitments, friends, and belongings that do not support our authenticity at midlife, we can reclaim our energy for better purposes.[17] "What is the real cost of 'going to lunch' with a person you'd rather not see?" she wonders.

Anthropologist Margaret Mead also valued the "emptying" that occurs when children leave home and women discharge their caregiving roles. She coined the term "postmenopausal zest" for the creativity and energy released at midlife.

We become selective, in part, because we realize, once we hit fifty, that we won't live forever. *How* we spend our time and *who* we invest in matters. We keep for life those friendships that bring us the most joy.

Fun Loving

Our friendships become lighthearted as we get older. We don't take ourselves as seriously as we did when we were younger. "I'm not nearly so easily hurt," one woman told me. "If I make two phone calls or invitations and get turned down, I don't go suck my thumb in a corner somewhere, thinking that 'Well, they don't like me anymore.' I just say, 'Well, they're busy. I'll keep trying.' "

Laughter seals friendships. When I asked one woman what attracted her to her best friend initially, she said, "We laughed a lot." And they still do. Another said, "If I can't laugh with someone, probably I'm not friends with her. There's a lot of laughter in all my relationships—just getting serious and talking about something deep and then finding the absurdity in it."

Laughter can heal, Norman Cousins, former editor of *The Saturday Review,* discovered during his recovery from a crippling disease. He later documented his findings in his best-selling book *Anatomy of an Illness.* Laughter among good friends has a similar effect. Only a good friend knows how to make you laugh when you're in the pits of despair. A good friend brings lightness at the darkest times. A good friend reminds us, especially as we get older and misfortunes befall us and our families, "This, too, shall pass. Keep your sense of humor."

Chapter Two

The Legacy of Our Mothers and Sisters

"We can only learn to love by loving."

Iris Murdoch

Meryl, a fifty-year-old married teacher, grew up in a family of women. An only child whose father died six months after her birth, Meryl was raised by her mother, the youngest of three sisters, who called each other eight to ten times a day. One, a widow, and the other, married to a man who worked long hours, lived a few blocks from Meryl and her mother.

"I grew up seeing women who cared about each other, consulted with each other, and collaborated with each other in so many ways," she recalls. "Having relationships with women is like breathing. So is talking on the phone. Just relating to people is a function of my personality but also the way I was raised."

She goes on: "My mom, who died five years ago at ninety, and I talked about everything and that was one of the advantages of how I grew up. (It had some weird aspects to it, too: My relationships with men were undeveloped because I didn't have a father.) My mom always talked to me as if I were her equal, even when I was five or six. She would talk about dynamics and people and friends and intuition. She cared about people and was a really good listener."

Meryl learned from her mother—through observation and by osmosis—that to be a good friend you must be a good listener. Her mother also taught her about intimacy. Meryl grew up seeing her mother interact with her sisters all day long. She observed the trio of sisters with rose-colored glasses, longing for such connections herself. Another woman might have wondered whether it was healthy for three sisters to be so enmeshed in each other's lives.

For better or worse, depending on your viewpoint, most of us do not have relationships with our mothers like Meryl's. But we all get messages from them about friendship: some spoken, some unspoken. We may choose to embrace or reject their messages, but few of us are able to avoid their influence. What we observed as children about our mothers and their friends (or lack thereof), how our mothers related to us growing up, and the nature of our adult mother-daughter connections all impact on us, and may affect our choice of friends and the way we relate to them. Our sisters, too, can have lasting effects on our ability to make friends, our need for companionship, and the nature of our voluntary connections.

A Model for Closeness

Social scientists and feminists continue to debate whether the mother-daughter relationship, often portrayed as the model for closeness, is the prototype of female friendships.[1] Our first experience with love and need, disappointment and hurt, the mother-daughter bond becomes a guide and model for loving and being, for expectations, needs, and hopes.[2] Little do we realize growing up that we will pattern our female friendships on that very first attachment.[3]

This crucial connection impacts on how we view all our relationships, says psychotherapist Susan Balis, MSS, author of *Beyond the Illusion: Choices for Children of Alcoholism.* "Female friendships bring out issues around the way we were nurtured, what we want to give, and how we structure the relationship. What you did or didn't get from your mother—unless you've worked that through—will color what you get from friends," she believes.

That doesn't mean we need to mend our relationships with our mothers before we can build solid alliances with our friends. Even at our age, the mother-daughter relationship ebbs and flows. But our friendships can help us work out unresolved issues with our mothers or give us what we didn't or couldn't get from them.

It's usually not necessary to go back and confront your mother eyeball to eyeball, however, because at this stage of life we've internalized so many mother-daughter issues. If you always expect people to disappoint you, for example, it doesn't really matter whether your mother does or doesn't at this point. You may unconsciously choose friends who disappoint you in an attempt to rework that original interaction. Or you may think you set up relationships so they won't disappoint you and then lo and behold . . . they do. But it's not necessary to challenge your mother today about how she disappointed you in the past. Hopefully at midlife you've reached a mature perspective on the parenting you received, so you're able to be more understanding and less angry. "She did the best she could," you might say, or, "I now understand why she acted the way she did."

At least one woman I interviewed, however, felt she needed to settle the score with her mother. Rita, fifty-two, and her mother, eighty, had a troubled relationship for years. Her mother constantly criticized Rita and blamed her for her two divorces. Rita also had difficulty making and sustaining friendships. Intuitively, she felt a connection existed between the two. She told me, "I have worked very hard on my relationship with my mom since I became fifty. I had a lot of anger and resentment toward her, but when I started going inside me, finding the place that felt good, I was able to approach her in a different way than I had before."

Rita continues, "Subconsciously I knew I had to go back and mend the fence with her before it was too late—if it was going to trickle down to anyone else. I had tried a couple of times before but maybe not wholeheartedly. She was very, very angry with me then, screamed and yelled, and kicked me out of her house, told me I had no right to confront her. But the anger and hatred were killing me."

Ironically, or perhaps not, Rita has developed her first genuine friendship with another woman in the last few years. Fawn, a thirty-four-year-old married woman who works in Rita's office, could not be more different from her. Says Rita, "She's very serious, quiet, and focused and I'm outgoing, flamboyant, and talkative." They balance each other and help one another stretch in new ways. Fawn helps Rita stay focused at work while Rita has introduced spirituality into Fawn's life.

Just how did Rita's improved relationship with her mother enable her to build a solid connection with a woman? It's complicated. Susan Balis explains, "Rita had learned to express some anger toward her mother, was able to tolerate her mother's anger back, realizing it didn't destroy her mother or herself. It would make sense that then she can risk a little more in a relationship, because she can get angry and know it's not the end of the world."

Rita's relationship with her mother needed a major overhaul.

Not every mother-daughter liaison needs such extensive repair. Sometimes we simply need to be aware of issues with our mothers so we can recognize when those same blind spots affect our friendships. Barbara, a therapist, felt Nina, a close friend, was extremely critical of her; she had to take "a little bite" out of each of her accomplishments. Barbara felt devastated by Nina's comments, but she also had enough presence of mind to wonder why she felt so shattered by such petty slights. "It was such a profound wound in me somewhere," Barbara recalls. "I was able to finally realize it was the mother wound. I could not get my mother's approval."

It's not surprising that Barbara overreacted to Nina's remarks because they brought back years of hearing her mother's biting accusations and then subsequently feeling angry and diminished. It's possible, however, that Nina's words were not as cutting as Barbara experienced them, but that she interpreted them that way because of how she views the world. She responded to Nina as if she were the critical mother. But Nina may not have been unduly harsh; Barbara may have been unduly sensitive. Whereas someone else would just shrug off her friend's comment, Barbara overreacted to it. On the other hand, it's also possible that Nina truly *was* critical, but because of Barbara's bias in this area, she didn't realize that Nina's own problems—insecurity or jealousy perhaps—prompted the criticism.

At other times we see our mothers' ways of relating to their friends in ourselves, and much as we want to behave differently, we can't break that pattern. Maureen, a fifty-one-year-old married woman from the Midwest, realized recently that she has difficulty reaching out and calling somebody or initiating plans. Her mother had had the same problem. "She had the tendency to sit back and wait for people to come to her. Part of it was because she was naturally shy and reserved. Then, too, she had no real strong need to reach out to people and let them know how important they were in her life, because she was surrounded by six brothers and sisters," Maureen notes. "The lessons Mom taught me I absorbed unconsciously and I'm not sure they were good ones. I had to overcome the mark she made on me to make my relationships more fruitful."

How did she go about doing that? "Painfully," she responds. With her oldest daughter's help. Tina, now twenty-seven, was an angry teenager. She neglected her schoolwork, hung out with a tough crowd, and mouthed off to her parents. When she totaled the family car, they all went to counseling. "When I was confronted with Tina's anger and a lot of her challenging statements, I began to recognize that there was another way of looking at life and my way didn't have to be the right way. It was just *my way*. I began changing—very slowly—at that point," Maureen acknowledges.

The experience with her daughter created ripples in her friendships. "I was always proud before. I would never share family stuff with friends. I had to be perfect," Maureen recalls. "But I was in so much pain, I had to reach out. My friends were there and no one looked at me as a failure as a mother."

Initiating, though, is still difficult for her. "I can take leadership roles in certain situations, but when it comes to inviting people to do things, I'm still a little bit hesitant," she admits. "I'm an introvert and I'm perfectly fine doing things by myself. That's part of it. Even though rationally I know it's not a rejection of me, if people turn me down, that knowledge takes a little bit longer to travel to my heart. So emotionally sometimes I just don't want to make myself vulnerable."

Mothers and Friends

"If women had a good or pretty good mother-daughter relationship, they would be more inclined to value female friends,"
says psychiatrist and author Jean Baker Miller. "On the other
hand, where there hasn't been a good relationship, sometimes female friends have really made a tremendous difference."

If you're close to your mother, you don't have *less* of a need
for friends. That connection makes it *more possible* to have
friends. Forming a positive, healthy bond with one woman enables
you to develop such ties with others. Once we learn how to es-
tablish such a relationship at home, we can take that knowledge
into the world. In actuality, the same attributes—trust, empathy,
caring, support, and shared intimacies—compose all good relationships, whether with a mother, friend, or husband.

Some women, however, who have a close relationship with their
mothers do seem to need friends less. Consider the woman whose
mother becomes her best friend after she has children, or the
woman who lives down the block from her mother or who talks
to her several times a day. These mothers and daughters do *seem*
sufficient onto themselves. But what is the nature of their relationship?

Several studies have shown a lack of openness or intimacy between middle-class mothers and their adult daughters. The same
finding held true in research of working-class women, although
they were more involved with their mothers. These daughters
needed their mothers' practical help for their survival. That situation did not necessarily foster positive associations, however. The
daughters considered their interactions routine and necessary;
some even called them boring.[4]

The mother-daughter relationship tends to be obligatory, unlike
friendships, which are voluntary. Mothers and friends serve dif-

ferent purposes, usually come from different generations, and bring different perspectives. Several studies have shown that even mother-daughter relationships identified as close did not have a high level of intimate confiding.[5] Many women don't talk to their mothers about marital conflicts because they don't want to worry them. Nor do they feel comfortable discussing their sex lives or sexual problems. Of the few women in my study who said they felt close to their mothers today, most still censored what they told them. They shared *somewhat* but not in the same depth or detail as they would with a close friend. "I wouldn't want to upset her," they told me. Or, "She doesn't need to know everything at her age." Having a close connection with your mother as an adult, while definitely something to be prized, does not preclude having good friends.

Positive Messages/Positive Role Models

Megan, a forty-eight-year-old homemaker married to a successful plastic surgeon with three daughters in their late teens, received only positive messages about friendship growing up. Some came in her mother's well-modulated voice over the fine china and sterling silver as they ate family dinners. Others she observed growing up in a household where if she said anything negative about someone, the next day she had to balance her critical remarks with three compliments.

"My family has always had the motto 'The more you share, the more you're blessed,' " Megan told me. "My mom was always the first one at somebody's house with a bowl of soup or bread. She always taught me to be really, really kind and nurturing and to look for the good in people. Friendships were always important to my mother and my family. We took time to nurture them. She always had people over for coffee, sent special cards. One of her friends loved roses, so every year for her birthday she'd go to her garden and pick a bouquet of roses. Never anything fancy, but a token that she thought about you and what you'd like."

Megan has adopted these values as her own. Like her mother, she is the first to send a card, bring a meal, or visit a sick friend. She feels grateful that she has several best friends and a larger circle of acquaintances. Although they rarely have conflicts, if something does bother her, she prays for guidance and asks God to help her see the other person's viewpoint. I didn't ask Megan about her relationship with her mother, but if I had, I'm sure she would have told me that she considers her mother one of her closest friends.

Megan's situation sounds almost too good to be true. I heard many other stories of women whose mothers also showed them by example how to be a good friend. With such positive models, these women developed their own long-lasting friendships with ease. However, in no way did this ensure that mother and daughter were close. Because a woman can develop close relations with *her* peers, it does not follow that she is able to nurture her own daughter. The older woman may not know how because *her* mother kept *her* distant. She may feel protective, as many of our mothers did, insisting that you don't share intimacies with the younger generation—even though at this point we are all adult women.

Kathryn, the woman introduced in the last chapter who moved from Connecticut to California with her husband a few years ago, believes her mother patterned a positive model of friendship, yet mother and daughter remain distant to this day. Kathryn remembers at six or seven years of age accompanying her mother to her best friend's house on Saturdays. As Kathryn played with her dolls, she observed the two women chatting and laughing for hours. Yet she and her mother never shared that kind of rapport when she was growing up or as adults. Kathryn believes their remote mother-daughter relationship prevented her from developing close ties with women until later in life.

Kathryn and her mother never developed an adult relationship, Kathryn contends, because her mother continues to "baby" her. "We are very different women. I have more of an intellectual approach to life than she does," Kathryn explains. "She and I have had this approach-avoidance relationship. When she distances, I want to be close. Then we come together and I get claustrophobic and pull away. She has made enormous emotional demands on me at times, and that has made me distance myself from her. I needed that independence from her, and that has prevented our being close."

In her twenties, Kathryn realized that all her close friends were men. Psychotherapy helped her accept her mother and also herself, as different from her mother. "Since then I'm much closer to women," she notes. "It was as if I was taking all my anger out on the female gender. When I was younger, my relationship with my mother definitely affected my friendships. Not so now."

Kathryn keeps in touch with old friends back in Connecticut through e-mail and phone calls. In California she has made several new friends by joining a church and volunteering at the local historical society. She feels good about the mix of old and new friends yet realizes that her mother's legacy will always be with her. "My mother's father passed away right before I was born, and she was very dependent on him. She lived two houses down from her parents, even though she was married and had a child. She really flipped out when her father died, and almost lost me in the pregnancy because she was so hysterical," Kathryn recalls.

"After I was born, she became extraordinarily depressed. As a result of that—talk about the influences of mothers on their children—for most of my life I have struggled with periods of depression, and I think her inability to be there for me as a mother created some of my distancing tendencies. When somebody gets too close, it alarms me a bit. It brings back those old memories. Those female relationships form your first reality, and my first reality was not being very close."

Like Kathryn, Ruth admired and envied her mother's friendships. Ruth never thought she'd have as many friends or be as popular. Time and again her mother told her that friendships are "worth fighting for." Ruth is the woman from the last chapter who solidified each of her friendships with a fight. That both mother and daughter use a combat metaphor for friendship indicates how fiercely committed they both feel to their inner circles.

Despite their similar outlook on friendship, Ruth and her mother had a rocky relationship for years. Three years ago, just as Ruth's son Jason turned thirteen, their relationship took a positive turn. Almost simultaneously Ruth and her mother realized how perilous the teenage years could be. "My mother felt both compassion for me as a mother—a lonely job, as she'd always said—and compassion for Jason, who needed to be understood. The same thoughts operated on me, but from the opposite direction," she says. "I remembered how awful it was to be a teenager at war with my mother and didn't want it to happen to me now. And I remembered now, with great regret, the pain I'd caused my mother by moving so far away from her."

Consequently, Ruth's mother became her ally; together they helped Jason navigate his way through adolescence. "That was a terrible period for me and my mother, so in a way my mother helped me by mothering me now," Ruth says. "It's very comforting to listen to my mother talk about my son in a nonthreatening way—'He'll be fine, he'll be okay'—just what you want a friend to say. This is the relationship my mother and I could only have dreamed of when I was a teenager."

Mixed Messages

I received conflicting communications from my mother about friendship. Verbally she told me not to reveal our concerns to anyone outside the family. When we discussed family matters at home, I heard, "This business stays here." Even when my mother and father planned a vacation—something not particularly private—they didn't discuss their arrangements with anyone outside the family until they had paid for their reservations. "When the plans are made, we'll tell people," my mother would say. Why? I wondered. "It's nobody's business," she'd reply. I never could figure that out, nor could she explain it any better.

Despite these verbal messages, however, growing up I observed that her friends mattered tremendously to her. She volunteered at the hospital with her friends, worked on synagogue projects with them, played cards together. But her Sunday-morning ritual stands out in my memory. After my father left to do paperwork at the store, she'd plop down on a chair next to the phone in her long bathrobe and, with a mug of black coffee in one hand and a Chesterfield in the other, talk to her friend Sylvia. Sometimes they talked over an hour and then mother would check in with her other friends; occasionally she'd call her mother.

There was no question, however, that my father always came first. She would never talk that long if he was around. Nor would she go out with a friend if she expected him home. Her friends, all married women with children, felt the same way. When my father died, she was sixty-two. Her friends, many also widows, rallied. Instantly, a support system blossomed. She and five or six friends trekked *en masse* to dinner, the movies, the theater, shopping. She also traveled with my father's cousin Charlotte, who in recent years had become a confidante.

Looking back, I realize how vital friends were to her throughout her entire life, but I wonder about the depth and nature of those relationships. Did she confide in her friends as we do today? I doubt it. Other women told me they had similar reservations about their mothers' friendships. Our mothers came from a generation that valued privacy. They drew a distinct line between family and friends and certainly did not air what they would consider their "dirty laundry" in public. I know my mother felt close to her friends and comfortable with them, but I can't imagine her discussing her fears or vulnerabilities with them. But perhaps it's not fair for me to say what she *didn't* get. Obviously, her friends gave her the comfort and support she needed. And she must have responded in kind because her friends adored her.

As adults, she and I shared little of our emotional lives. We talked about the kids or the house or her activities or travels. We discussed what was happening in our lives, not our feelings about these events. I never discussed with her how I felt about being a mother—something she could have related to. She never told me how it felt to grow old or become sick. Even after my father died and I called often to check in, she always told me she was "fine." Of course, I had a responsibility for the quality of our relationship, too, but I never felt she'd welcome emotional sharing. If I complained about something, I'd get a flip quip—"That's life, bub"—not the empathy I yearned for. She had little tolerance for ambivalence or nuances. I know she saw me as a competent, independent adult but we never talked the way I do today with my friends and my twenty-six-year-old daughter.

Ironically, about ten years ago, shortly after my mother's death, I began opening up to friends in a different kind of way. I felt less of a need to appear composed and collected, more comfortable sharing my vulnerabilities, and, in fact, yearned to relate emotionally and honestly. My reaction makes me wonder: Was I unconsciously holding back all these years, still saving myself for her, hoping we would eventually connect? Or maybe her death freed me to relate differently (i.e., emotionally) with other women.

Perhaps. It may be just a coincidence that she died at a developmental point when I needed my peers. At age forty-four, I cared less what others thought, had little need to impress, and focused on doing what *I* required for myself. A family crisis compelled me to reach out. I hungered for connection as never before. The fact is, if she had been alive I probably would not have confided in her. Nor would she have been able to hear my pain and give me the comfort I needed.

But maybe my mother gave me a gift after all. Watching her talk to her friends all those Sundays provided a model that allowed me to reach out to my friends when I needed them most.

Rewriting Negative Scripts

A number of women told me they received only negative verbal messages from their mothers about friendship, that their mothers had no real friends, and that they had difficulty forming close ties with their mothers as adults. Without role models in any sense of the word, these women worked extra hard to develop and sustain friendships over the years. Two of these women's stories represent how women can move beyond the negative messages they received from their mothers and either build meaningful friendships of their own or alter the bond with their mothers. These transformations, which came after years of loneliness and isolation, occurred at midlife when women attain the emotional maturity and distance to view their mothers more realistically but also more compassionately.

Nora, a fifty-year-old divorced biologist who never had children, grew up in a Catholic, middle-class home as the only daughter. She longed for a sister. Her mother, who Nora said had no friends, seemed more connected to Nora's three aunts than to her.

Nora developed a clarity about her relationship with her mother, who is deceased, over the last six months and realized for the first time how that impacted on her ability to make friends. The realization came about, she believes, partly because of her mature perspective and partly because she had developed an inner circle of friends. "I now have support, warmth, and belonging to face my childhood as it was. For me to switch from family to friends has been a big shift. I heard, 'You go to family.' That message held me back. I learned not to count on anyone outside the family. In graduate school and high school I did have friends, but this feels different: It's more deliberate on all sides. We say things to each other, like, 'You're really important to me.' "

She continues, "My recognition of how far my mother was from me came at the same time that my relationships were deepening. It's not a coincidence. Developing friends makes me realize what I was missing with my mother. But it makes me sad and horrified that it's taken me so long. My relationship with my mother was dry. I didn't see it for what it was. I reached out a lot [to her] but I didn't have a model. I always had distance and disappointment and an inflexibility: This is how it is. I didn't *have* a relationship, so how could I replicate it?" she wonders aloud.

Nora set out to develop a set of friends by consciously selecting women who shared her two passions: photography and hiking. "I was looking for people who really love what I love," she explained. Relationships with two women she knew casually intensified as their conversation and activities centered on their mutual interests. She also developed new friendships with several women she met at a photography club and on a hiking trip.

Perhaps her friendships also deepened because she was more giving now? Not at all, she says. "If anything, I'm less giving. I'm not needing friendships as much as I used to. All my relationships—with men, too—are secondary to my relationship with myself. I expect less and more is possible, because I'm freer to receive or not receive and not be destroyed by it."

For the first time bonds of friendship feel mutual. When she was going through a bad spell, one friend reassured her, "I'm planning to grow old with you." No one had ever said that to her.

For a long time Nora emulated her mother's model of detachment. Yet at midlife, for a reason she cannot explain, she felt a need and desire to develop friends, and did. They, in turn, gave her the support and strength to face her past. She recognized the barrenness of her relationship with her mother and the isolation she had felt without close friends. It would have been too threatening to acknowledge this at a younger age when she didn't have a support system. The knowledge would have left her bereft.

It's possible, however, that Nora's past was not as bleak as she remembers, says psychotherapist and author Susan Balis. "The fact that she can take from other women tells me she got something somewhere from someone. It could have been a grandmother or she could have gotten a little more from her mother than she realized. Today, with all the fuss about victims, everybody exaggerates the bad. Even an alcoholic mother isn't always drunk, but the daughter can't remember the other times." Nonetheless, Nora governed her life on *her* perception of her past.

Helene, who grew up in a working-class family, remembers that her mother had a few acquaintances at church and in the neighborhood but no real friends. Even today, her mother cannot name a special friend. Like Nora, Helene grew up in an environment that prohibited her from discussing its business outside their home. "Outsiders" received a condensed or altered version of the facts. When her father, who was an alcoholic, had a physical breakdown because of his drinking, her mother told her friends he had a heart problem; no one questioned her story.

Unlike Nora, Helene rejected her mother's way and rebelled against the family's dictum as a teen. "I remember thinking, 'I can't follow you. I can't do it like you.' It wasn't that there was propaganda slipped under your door to tell you to rebel. It was just in the air in the sixties. So many obvious things to rebel against but also a lot of subtleties that we weren't going to do the same way our mothers did—like friendship. They didn't even share when one of their kids went awry. That was all well hidden."

Helene developed close friends in college and today prizes several twenty-year-old friendships. Her bond with her mother, however, remained distant and impersonal until four years ago. Helene will never forget the moment that transformed their relationship. She recalls, "Mom was visiting and we had gone shopping. I was about to turn the key in my lock, and she said, 'There's something . . .' and she started to cry. I said, 'Something what?' " Her mother told her that she had been molested by a family friend from the time she was seven until she was twelve and had never told anyone. She only told Helene now, because she had been plagued with nightmares since she watched a television show on incest three days before.

Helene continues. "After she cried and we hugged—it was a very close moment—I asked her if she would let me be that candid with her about things in my life. She said, 'You weren't molested, were you?' I said, 'No, but, Mom, this is what women do.' She said, 'You can tell me anything.' "

By revealing a secret she had buried for more than seventy years, Helene's mother reshaped their relationship. Helene also deserves credit for being open and responsive to her mother. She accepted her mother's confidence in an empathic way. She also used the situation to educate her mother about the ways women share intimate, sometimes painful, things. She gave her mother permission to continue sharing, which opened the door for her to be honest and open with her mother as well. Although Helene doesn't tell her eighty-three-year-old mother everything, by Helene's account, they have a mutual, adult connection for the first time in fifty years.

Sisters: A Mixed Blessing

I learned my first lessons in intimacy from my younger sister Anne, not my mother. By day she annoyed me. I didn't like her hanging around when my friends came over; I resented her constant questions and nosiness. But at night, in our darkened bedroom, with just the glow of the nightlight, we became allies. After we said good night to our parents, we'd lie in bed on our stomachs, pillows scrunched under our chests, and yak. School, friends, the 'rents (as we called our parents). We covered it all. On and on, we'd gab and giggle until eventually mother would yell from the living room, "Enough already." We'd simmer down and whisper until eventually one of us fell off to sleep.

Little did I know at the time, those late night tête-à-têtes provided the training ground for my friendships and Anne's. I learned how to share, to listen, to trust another female. And yet I think that my mother's verbal messages about not divulging family business and her superficial relationships with her friends overpowered what I learned with Anne, because it took me a long time to truly open up with other women. Interestingly, Mother's messages did not have the same effect on Anne, who is four years

younger. In talking with me recently she said she didn't even remember the warnings so imprinted on my psyche. She came of
age in the midst of the women's movement, embraced its openness
and camaraderie among women, and belonged to consciousness-
raising groups where she and her friends "let it all hang out,"
much to my mother's horror.

That relationships within our family of origin influence our
friendships seems obvious, yet little research has focused on the
subject. "It's hard to untangle the impact of sisters from that of
parents," Marian Sandmaier, author of *Original Kin: The Search
for Connection Among Adult Sisters and Brothers,* told me. "There
can be a link between friendship and sisters, particularly in those
close in age, and their experiences with each other in terms of
closeness, competition, distance, and expectations. A woman's
role in the family vis-à-vis her sisters can also affect her friendships." Though her sister was older, Marian had a more dominant
personality. "I have a tendency to be the center of attention. I'm
aware of this and I try not to let that interfere in my friendships.
I consciously try to value other people and make a point to know
in detail what's going on in their lives, so there's a give-and-take."

The roots of this pattern date back to high school, when her
family moved from New Jersey to California. "My sister was the
person I could rely on. But I was always the one my father valued
the most and gave more attention to, so there's always lurking for
me the guilt and the worry that that's going to happen again in
my friendships: that I'm going to hog the limelight and drive my
friends away," she comments.

Cynthia, a sixty-year-old married teacher from Washington,
D.C., illustrates how an unhealthy pattern of relating to a sister
can be repeated in a friendship. Despite their personality differences, Cynthia and her older sister Sue have always been able to
talk about everything. An extrovert and risk taker, Cynthia iden-

tified more with her father, while Sue is more introverted and withdrawn, like their mother. Cynthia and her father, who passed away ten years ago, always "did" for her mother and sister. During a recent trip to Dallas to visit her mother and sister, Sue needed to call a friend. "Oh, would you call her?" Sue begged her younger sister.

Cynthia told me, "We spent our lives like that. I went through one period where I thought, no, I'm not going to be manipulated to do things she can do for herself. Now sometimes I find myself doing them by choice: If it's that hard for her, why not? She's not going to change at this point. I had to take my stand and let her know I wasn't always going to do it her way just to protect her. I tried to work through it and then dropped it."

Cynthia tried not to participate in her sister's dependency-and-helplessness dance but was unsuccessful. No doubt Cynthia felt outnumbered and overpowered, since her mother manipulated her in the same way. Cynthia was the odd woman out in a triangle with her mother and sister. This often happens, according to family therapy theory, when two family members deflect tensions between them onto a third member.[6] On the one hand, Cynthia deserves credit for extricating herself from the triangle by leaving Dallas years ago. It would have been better, however, if she could have resolved the issue at home rather than running from it. Each time she returns to Dallas, her mother and sister lure Cynthia into the caretaker role again. Cynthia says she accepts her sister for who she is today, which may be a way for Cynthia to rationalize her anger.

A few years ago Cynthia noticed that she would put herself out for certain friends but they wouldn't reciprocate; she would end up feeling hurt or angry. Once she recognized this familiar pattern, she abruptly ended these alliances. Today she feels proud that she has only reciprocal friendships. Again, Cynthia broke ties

with her friends rather than staying in the relationships and confronting the troublesome issue. Like many women, Cynthia has
difficulty asserting herself with those close to her.

Meg's situation, on the other hand, shows how a tangled tie
with a sister can sabotage friendships in a much more pervasive
way. In her case, her older sister's presence hung over her childhood like a dark storm cloud. A happy, well-adjusted little girl,
Meg felt she could not express her exuberance at home because
it would upset Lisa, a serious, unpopular child who gained the
attention of the entire family by being negative. At Meg's birthday
parties, Lisa would refuse cake, saying she was not hungry. If Meg
told a joke, Lisa would sit silently and glower.

"It was always 'poor Lisa,' 'poor Lisa,' " Meg, a fifty-one-year-
old human resources manager, recalls, mimicking her mother.
Meg could recall only one positive aspect of their childhood liaison: At three or four, she occasionally crawled in bed with her
big sister if she had a bad dream.

Meg said, "I was constantly feeling guilty and sorry for her. She
couldn't feel any joy for me and I couldn't allow myself to feel
joy either." Lisa didn't date in high school and was not invited to
a prom, so Meg eased her own guilt by going with someone she
didn't like, rather than her boyfriend. That way it felt more like
a responsibility.

Meg felt such an obligation to attach herself to Lisa first and
foremost that for years she felt guilty even *having* friends. "Lisa
tried to quash me because she couldn't be that way herself. I
generalized that to my friendships. I feel I have to be real careful
and subdued with a new friend. I always try to please," she says.
"There was also an element of withholding with my sister, so I
never trusted that women wouldn't withhold from me. I always
felt I was walking on eggshells. I felt judged, like I had to toe the
line or pay the consequences."

To this day Meg feels a burden to keep her friends happy and not shine too much herself. "I felt I had to hide parts of myself from my sister, so I was real cautious about who I let know me. If I leaned too heavily or expressed myself too much, I would throw off the balance. If I was too successful, I thought no one would like me. I had to be fine. I can bring a problem into the relationship if I'm okay with it, but if I really, really need someone, I'm very uncomfortable. Mostly I don't invest at all very deeply." Today she feels secure only with old friends whom she met in high school and college.

After their father's death five years ago, Lisa exploded at Meg, accusing her of having it all—being pretty, talented, and bright. "Ever since I realized that jealousy motivated Lisa and that I wasn't bad, I've relaxed some. It's sad because neither of us knows the other. Today we are beginning to accept each other, but she'll never understand me," says Meg. "Since Mom died last year, all we have is each other. She's not going to change, nor am I. The closeness we have is complicated and full of rough spots but we are each other's only family."

That sad realization, which often comes at midlife, can bring a new perspective to our connections with our sisters. Relationships can change. Maturity, acceptance, and forgiveness can alter sibling ties. Sisters who had limited, but not necessarily negative, impact on us as we were growing up can bring solace and even pleasure later in life. Norma told me how her younger sister Betty always kept her on a pedestal, which distanced them for years. Their father died when they were both in their forties, and Norma fell apart—in front of Betty, which made her realize that her big sister wasn't perfect after all. Recognizing Norma's frailties allowed Betty to comfort her at the time and, later, to develop more realistic expectations of her. Norma, in turn, felt accepted as a human being, not as an idol, and began sharing more of her feelings and difficulties with Betty. As they become reacquainted as adult women, their relationship feels more like a special friendship.

Martha, the oldest of four sisters, says they weren't very intimate with each other or their mother growing up. "Don't show me your pain" was their family's unwritten message. Recently, however, they all underwent family therapy following the arrest of a sister for driving under the influence of alcohol. This process forced them to connect and communicate with each other in a more open way. "That's probably one of the best things I've ever experienced," Martha told me. "I think that also might make some of my friendships feel less real because this stuff we're doing is so real. I never feel like I'm alone. I always know I can call on any of my sisters."

What could be better than having a sister who is a friend? Many would say, "Having a friend who feels like a sister." A lot of women used terminology of kinship to describe their closest friends: "She's like family to me," or "I love her like a sister." This is considered the highest compliment and yet beneath the surface of these idealized familial connections lurks the specter of conflict and competition. Today we understand, expect, and certainly talk freely about sibling rivalry. But the issues that separate us from other women—hurt, jealousy, anger, and competition—remain some of the most difficult for women to acknowledge, discuss, and handle, even at midlife.

Chapter Three

Challenges of Closeness

"If thou hast opened thy mouth against thy friend, fear not; for there may be a reconciliation: except for upbraiding, or pride, or disclosing of secrets, or a treacherous wound: for these things every friend will depart."

Ecclesiastes

Shirley MacLaine and Anne Bancroft, friends and rivals, dominate the movie *The Turning Point*. Elegant and stunning Emma, played by Anne Bancroft, devoted her life to her dancing career and has become a world-class ballerina. Dowdy Deedee (Shirley MacLaine) married another dancer, moved to Oklahoma, had three children, and opened a dance studio. The two women, estranged for years, reunite at midlife when Emma's troupe plays Oklahoma City.

When Emma offers Deedee's daughter an opportunity to dance with her in New York City, Deedee accompanies her for the summer. Old conflicts, which smoldered for years, flare up. Throughout the movie, Deedee's anger and jealousy flash out in sarcasm, stinging comments, and tears. A catfight between Emma and Deedee caps the movie. In high heels and long gowns, two grown women yell, slap, and spank each other, flinging purses and slinging epithets—"liar, user, bitch"—until they exhaust themselves.

Good drama? Perhaps. But that scene also stereotypes women's friendships, trivializing them as petty, catty, and insubstantial. While the clash between homemaker and career woman, circa 1977, seems outdated today, jealousy, anger, and competitiveness still plague women's friendships at the turn of the twenty-first century. These feelings are difficult to acknowledge and tricky to handle—no matter what our age. In fact, some of the examples in this chapter sound reminiscent of the way we handled spats with our best buddies in fourth grade. Others offer mature solutions to age-old conflicts. Risking a constructive confrontation, while definitely a challenge, can boost our self-esteem and strengthen our connections to women we care about.

Two Sides of the Coin

When women don't manage their anger well they fit into one of two categories, according to psychologist Harriet Lerner, Ph.D., author of *The Dance of Anger.* "Some women may avoid anger and conflict entirely and fit the societal stereotype of the 'nice lady.' Others may get angry with ease, but getting angry gets nowhere or even makes things worse." In a society that discourages female anger, Lerner notes that women who engage in ineffective fighting, complaining, and blaming may be called "bitches" or any number of pejorative labels, and that the negative words that depict women who do speak out are more than cruel sexist stereotypes. "Women who are labeled 'bitches,'" Lerner adds, "are often blocked from identifying and speaking clearly to the real issues."

That was not true for Emma and Deedee, because when they cooled down, they shared intimate feelings both had harbored for decades. Deedee waited twenty years for Emma to acknowledge that she had been threatened by Deedee's talent as a dancer. Emma revealed that she would have done anything to oust Deedee from the competition and, indeed, may have goaded her into marrying before Deedee felt ready.

"Nice ladies," on the other hand, stay silent. They become self-critical, tearful. Fearful of their own anger and of altering the status quo, they say nothing. They give in and go along, their fury building internally. Unlike "bitches," who get a bad rap from society for being unfeminine and unmaternal, our culture praises "nice ladies" for their calm, pleasing demeanor. Although "nice ladies" and "bitches" appear very different, they represent two sides of the same coin, says Dr. Lerner. Both ways of handling anger leave women feeling helpless, powerless, and stuck.[1]

I'm Mad As Hell But . . .

Not all women handle their anger poorly, especially at midlife. Of the fifty women I interviewed, only two, who are best friends, reported that they had a screaming match with each other. About half my sample told me they deal with conflicts directly in a mature, assertive way. Many of these women believe they developed these skills as they aged, that they would not have had the confidence to confront a friend ten or fifteen years ago. The other half, the "nice ladies," back off, swallow their feelings, pretend the issue doesn't matter, or bring in a third friend to mediate or vent to, much as they did in grade school.

Judy, a fifty-two-year-old homemaker, is not comfortable speaking directly with people who anger her. When her friend Mia and her husband started selling bulk frozen foods, Judy told her she wasn't interested but Mia pressured her on the phone anyway: "Could we *please* come and talk to you?" One day Mia showed up on Judy's doorstep. Rather than tell Mia how she felt, Judy called several other friends to discuss what happened. She says she felt better after venting. One of her friends then called Mia and told her to lay off. A few days later Judy received a note from Mia saying, "I'm sorry if I pressured you. I wouldn't want to do anything to disturb our friendship."

What's wrong with enlisting a third friend? I asked Harriet Lerner in a telephone interview. Judy got what she wanted, didn't she? "It's best to be able to talk directly to the person you're angry at," Lerner said. "It can be very helpful to talk to another friend first, particularly if she is a clear thinker who can help you get a new perspective, or make a plan about how to approach the person you have the conflict with. But the real challenge is to deal directly with the important people in your life rather than through a third party. It makes for a cleaner and more thorough resolution of the issue."

If, however, you can't be in the same room with a friend without the two of you becoming so volatile that neither of you will listen to the other, then the presence of a third party can help calm things down. "That would be a step," Lerner acknowledged, "but I would hope it would just be a step before you can talk directly."

Barbara, a therapist, needed to enlist her friends as mediators. When Abby, whom she had known for fifteen years, ridiculed the title of Barbara's new book, she silently fumed. She could not confront Abby alone; she felt the issue was too "loaded." She knew she'd explode. It reminded her of how her mother would criticize her for bringing home an exam score of *only* ninety-five.

Barbara brought in two close friends, who also knew Abby, as intermediaries. She told them, "I don't want to talk *about* Abby but I can't seem to face her with this." The next week they all sat down around Barbara's dining-room table. The woman acting as moderator said, "We have something we need to talk about. Barbara wants to say something to you, Abby." Barbara said her piece. Abby apologized, saying she had not intended to hurt her. She acknowledged that she had grown up with two brothers who teased a lot and sometimes she didn't realize when she had gone too far. Sheepishly, she admitted that she was a little envious of Barbara's recent book. "It was powerful stuff," concedes Barbara, who says her relationship with Abby is back on track.

Although it would have been better for Judy and Barbara to express their anger directly to the person who irritated them, at least they dealt with it. The other "nice ladies" in my sample told me they bit their tongues. One woman, who grew up in a confrontational household, said, "I don't have the time or strength for a confrontation. [If I'm angry] I just don't contact her for a while." Another rationalized, "We have no conflicts. I don't allow there to be any. My friendship is more important than any momentary annoyance."

A so-called momentary annoyance, however, may have lasting effects. If not dealt with, anger can undermine a friendship. If you've ever seethed at your sister or mother and not uttered a word, you know how those feelings can gnaw away at you and erode a relationship. A friendship that harbors silent anger may survive, but at what cost?

Like many women, Judy and Barbara are operating under a false premise: that they will lose the friendship if they voice their anger. The truth is, we do not have to choose between friendship and conflict. Solid friendships can weather differences and, indeed, become strengthened by the resolution of conflict.

Before you confront a friend about feeling angry, try to clarify your own thoughts and feelings. Determine the real issue: What about the situation makes you angry? If you can, try to separate your issues from your friend's and analyze the way this situation developed. Then attempt to figure out what you want to accomplish by the encounter, what you hope will change, and what you will and will not tolerate. Once you have explored these issues, you will be in a better position to decide whether to speak up. Whether or not you decide to challenge your friend, this process will allow you to calm down and prevent you from blowing up, venting, and blaming.[2]

Keeping Up with Ms. Jones

Competition disguises a need for attention and a desire for recognition. It is about us, not the other person, and stems from how we feel about ourselves. We want someone to listen to us and appreciate how it's been for us, say psychotherapists Luise Eichenbaum and Susie Orbach in *Between Women: Love, Envy and Competition in Women's Friendships*. Fear that we won't be listened to, that we'll become invisible, fuels the competition.[3] The woman who is competitive struggles with feelings of inadequacy and self-doubt, but she feels too ashamed to admit these, so she flips the negative into its opposite: I can do better than you.[4]

The roots of competition lie in our attachment to our mothers. Sharing the same gender, we recognize our similarities but know we must separate to become our own person—clearly one of the hardest developmental tasks we face. Boys and men don't have this difficulty because they are physically and biologically "the other" from day one, which produces a different mother-child relationship. As Jean Baker Miller and others have stressed: *We learn who we are by connecting with others, while men define themselves by distinguishing themselves from others.*[5] Thus, competition—really a form of separation—enhances a man's sense of self while it threatens a woman's.

Men play out their rivalry openly: sparring on the racquetball court, comparing investments or automobiles, jockeying for position in conversation. Men see themselves as individuals in a hierarchical social order in which they are either "one-up or one-down," according to linguist Deborah Tannen, Ph.D. She explains, "In this [man's] world, conversations are negotiations in which people try to achieve and maintain the upper hand if they can, and protect themselves from others' attempts to put them down and push them around."[6] Women, in contrast, use conversations to connect, and gain confirmation and support.

For all these reasons, women have a much harder time acknowledging and owning their competitive feelings, let alone expressing them. But they still exist and seep out in subtle and not-so-subtle ways, such as the criticism Barbara's friend leveled at her book title.

Knowing all this, I still was not prepared for the results of my survey. In the preliminary questionnaire, I asked women to identify the areas in which they felt competitive with their friends. The choices included children, money, clothes, career, weight, and partners. "Not competitive" was also an option. A full 74 percent of my sample labeled themselves as non competitive.

I raised the issue again in interviews to verify the survey results. Women hemmed and hawed. I heard such comments as: "I knew you weren't going to believe this, but I'm not competitive with my friends." "I read the question three times but I couldn't think of an area where I was competitive." "I'm afraid that I'm sugar-coating something or not facing it, but I can't think of any great competition right now." "I am a competitive person, but I play it out on the tennis court." The few women who acknowledged competitive feelings said they centered on friends who had more fulfilling careers or more successful children than theirs.

Were three-quarters of my sample truly not competitive or were they in denial? At midlife we feel more sure of ourselves, have reached some acceptance of our lot in life, and take more responsibility for our happiness than we did at a younger age. We're less likely to blame others for our failures and more willing to acknowledge regrets and stand accountable for paths not taken. In our twenties and thirties, we competed for men, for being the best dressed, even for being the worst off. "You'll never believe what my boyfriend/husband did/said," one woman will say. "That's nothing," another replies as she tops her pal's tale.

Thus, I believe competition between women does lessen considerably as we age, but not to the extent reported in my survey. These numbers do not accurately depict what happens between women. Rather, they reflect women's difficulty in *owning* their competitive feelings.

Jean Baker Miller confirmed my theory. "Competition is one of the hardest things for women to admit to and know how to deal with. But the reason women find competition so difficult differs from the reasons with men," she believes. "It isn't that women can't stand to be second best or less than second best. With women, it's a question of exclusion. If I'm not as good as her, if I don't have as good a job or as clean a house, I'll be known as some 'schlub' that people won't want to include."

She continues, "Women may feel competitive in order to be included and accepted. I think it's *that* that troubles women about competition. It definitely gets less as you get older, but it's still there—without its really sharp edge."

Inclusion matters to women. When included, we feel connected to one another. We gain our identities from such connections. Exclusion suggests isolation and rejection. Feeling disconnected and separate creates such discomfort and disharmony internally that we feel compelled to deny our competitive feelings.

Green With . . .

While competition concerns our sense of inadequacy, envy reflects our own desires and wanting. These emotions, too, generate discomfort as well as shame. Whereas we deny our competitive feelings in an effort to disown them, we try to dismiss envy by projecting it onto a friend. Say you can't afford a vacation and a good friend takes off for Paris. Envy is a natural response. Her going reminds you of how much you yearn to travel. But it's painful to look at your own situation—why you can't go. The more you dwell on it, the worse you feel. You question: What's wrong with me? Why can't I earn more so I can travel, too? How much easier to discard those uncomfortable feelings by casting them onto a friend. "Oh, going away again?" you remark sarcastically. Or you offer a guilt-inducing comment: "I guess you don't have to worry about money."

You try to bring your friend down so you can feel better. It's not that you wish to take away what she has or that you want her to have less, but her *having* awakens your deficiency and your desire for more. Envy allows us to project our feelings, so we experience them as less internally disruptive and threatening.[7] We don't have to change because *she's* the one with the problem.

Although I did not inquire about envy in my preliminary survey, in interviews I observed that women felt more comfortable about acknowledging feeling envious than feeling competitive. Perhaps envy is a safer emotion. Traditionally, envy has been associated with women although in a negative way. Competition feels more foreign, more male, and may generate more discomfort, because our society condemns women when they exhibit so-called masculine traits, such as assertiveness.

When we have the courage to recognize our own envy and handle it openly, this process can draw us closer to a friend, rather than driving a wedge between us. Sandi, a teacher, acknowledged to her best friend, Kim, how fortunate Kim was and how Sandi's own life came up lacking at times. "Sometimes I have a tinge of envy when her kids come home and I haven't seen mine for a while. I might be able to say, 'Oh, you're so lucky to have the kids around,' " Sandi told me. "Or when she had a lot of career activity going on and I was in a slump, I could say, 'It's so nice you're so busy. I feel so bad. I have nothing going on.' Or when my relationships were not going well, and I'd be around her and her husband, there'd be a loneliness for me." Sandi put her pain on the table. This allowed the two friends to discuss Sandi's longings and unhappiness.

Barbara, who has an undergraduate degree in sociology, envies Deena, who has a Ph.D. Her acknowledgment of her feelings generated a different result. "I was tongue-tied around Deena, because she had this incredible education. She was so bright I was uncomfortable around her at first—not because she had a problem with it. Because I did," Barbara admits. "Anytime I'm envious I need to look at that undeveloped part of myself, because that other person is a mirror for something that I need to tend to. It's like falling in love. We fall in love with the qualities we don't have in our own personality."

Barbara did not wish to take away Deena's graduate education; she wanted her own. Seeing how confident and articulate Deena was made Barbara recognize her own deficiencies as well as her desire for more schooling, which she had been vaguely aware of for a long time. Rather than lashing out at Deena, she turned her envy into energy and decided to seriously consider what she needed to do to go back to school.

When we're able to recognize envy as Barbara and Sandi did, we can transform it to work for us in a positive way. Once in touch with our own longings, we can choose to act on them or not. We can try to understand and resolve the inhibitions that prevent us from pursuing our goals.[8] It also helps to recognize how societal roles and traditional scripts for women restrict us.

Sometimes, however, we can become so consumed with what we *don't* have that we fail to appreciate what we do. Midlife is a time to take stock and be grateful for our gifts. We all have accomplishments we're proud of as well as disappointments and disillusionments. Perhaps you don't have a Ph.D. but have raised two healthy, independent children. Maybe you can't afford to travel but your home is a haven for a close circle of single friends. If we're lucky, we can discuss these issues with a good friend who will help us better understand our emotions, concentrate on the positives, and find the balance we seek.

Burned by a Pal

Mention "Linda Tripp" and women from Boston to Berkeley cringe. In case you've been living in a cave and don't recognize her name, Tripp, forty-eight, secretly tape-recorded telephone conversations with Monica Lewinsky, the White House intern who had an affair with President Clinton, and then went public with the tapes. Creating a mini-scandal of its own, Tripp's betrayal of Lewinsky left women aghast: "How could she?" "With friends like that . . ." One commentary writer for the *Philadelphia Inquirer* labeled Tripp "the Queen of Bad Friendship." Indeed, her actions represent the most detestable and most feared crime a friend can commit.

When we confide in a friend, we assume she will honor our confidences and not repeat them. We trust her implicitly. That's not to say we haven't all been burned by a pal at one time or another. Remember the fourth-grade buddy who promised to keep your deepest secret then blabbed to the whole gang at recess? Or the eighth-grade chum who swore she wouldn't breathe a word of your crush on the class president and then squealed in study hall? At midlife, though, we're supposed to be grown-ups. We don't do that kind of thing anymore. Many of us have invested years and years in friendships. We take them seriously and particularly now, as our connections deepen, they matter tremendously. A betrayal can be devastating.

Envy, greed, revenge, fear of another's anger or of personal loss can lead to betrayals. The need to avoid or escape blame or disapproval, or to cover up a mistake, can also drive a betrayal. Most often betrayals result from a combination of several subtle motives.[9] In fact, you may never find out what caused a friend to stab you in the back. Even if she offers an explanation, it may not be the real reason.

Meryl, a teacher with two college-age children, told me that Jennifer, one of her best friends, lies to her repeatedly. In one instance, they agreed to register their daughters, then in high school, for the soccer team, which Meryl did. Jennifer led her to believe that she would do the same but never did. When Meryl questioned her at each step in the process, Jennifer had a ready excuse: She was "just going to do it," she forgot the registration card at work, she left it at her mother's. When Meryl confronted Jennifer about why she lied, Jennifer cried and apologized but never offered an explanation. Meryl believes Jennifer grew up lying. "That's just the way she is," she explains.

Occasionally Meryl resorts to "testing" Jennifer—another indication of her distrust—to see if she's telling the truth. She always fails the test. Jennifer continues to lie, while Meryl stays in a friendship in which trust has been destroyed. She explains her rationale. "It would be more difficult to have a parting than to have a problematic thing together. This is the better alternative,"

Meryl concedes. "I've made a decision to accept a major flaw. I'm not perfect. This is a huge imperfection but I think the positives outweigh the negatives."

Meryl is not blind. She has carefully thought out her decision to remain in this friendship, although you or I might have made a different choice. After balancing the pros and cons, she decided the positives, which include their long history, Jennifer's ability to keep a confidence and support Meryl in tough times, compensate for Jennifer's failings.

When someone breaks a trust, you have several options, says Jane Greer, Ph.D., a marriage and family therapist and former adjunct assistant professor at Adelphi University School of Social Work. You can confront the person directly about the betrayal. You can avoid the confrontation but change the way you relate to her. Or you can walk away from the relationship. But, says Dr. Greer, "You cannot ignore a breach of trust. The price, in terms of your self-confidence and self-esteem, is just too high." There is no guarantee, however, that confrontation will bring resolution. But if you push the issue aside, ignore it, or try to forget it, the unfinished business will continue to haunt you.[10] In Meryl's case, she did confront Jennifer about lying, but the confrontation did not stop the behavior. After careful consideration, Meryl has chosen *not* to walk away from the relationship, but Jennifer's lying definitely does haunt their friendship.

Rebecca, a stockbroker who has been stung by her friend Toby's gossiping behind her back time and again, chose not to confront her or end the alliance. Instead, she altered the way she relates to Toby. Rebecca takes care not to reveal any personal information that she doesn't want repeated. "That feels 'yucky' to me. I have to be careful, thinking, 'She'll say this about me because she says other things about other people,' " Rebecca admits. "So I just edit what I say, which doesn't make it the best friendship, even though we are close. If someone has diarrhea of the mouth, you can't really change that person." Rebecca has accepted her friend and has chosen to stay in the relationship for her own reasons, as Meryl did.

In contrast, Helene, an accountant, ended an alliance after Emmy, a friend from college, spread rumors about her. When Helene landed several large accounts, she bought a Lexus and joined a country club. Emmy invented stories that Helene made a fortune through shady real-estate deals. Helene confronted her but the sniping continued. When it happened again, Helene said to her, "It might be better if we just take a sabbatical from each other." Emmy didn't object. Helene felt she had to "cut off the information highway." The less Emmy knew, the less she could use against her. If Helene bumps into her at a party, they chat briefly and go their separate ways.

Although Helene understands that jealousy probably motivated Emmy's behavior, she could not tolerate it. No matter what Emmy said in own her defense, Helene decided her actions spoke louder than her words. She needed to break off contact.

If a friend has betrayed you and you still want to preserve the relationship, consider following the three-step coping strategy recommended by Dr. Greer:[11]

1. Determine the Motive. Describe objectively what happened and then ask your friend what transpired from her point of view. Be curious and listen without condemning.

2. Express Your Feelings Clearly. Talk about yourself and how you feel about the betrayal. Use "I" statements. You might say, "When you lied to me, I felt . . ." Try to avoid "you" statements, such as "You are such a gossip," that inflame.

3. Set Limits. Focus on the actions you want taken and the behaviors you will no longer tolerate. You might say, "If you continue to lie, I cannot see you anymore." Or, "If I catch you spreading rumors one more time, that's it for our friendship."

If your friend admits her transgression and apologizes, you must then try to forgive her and move on. If, however, she reacts with denials, put-downs, or defiance, try to remain calm, restate your position, and set your boundary again. You may need to call a time-out from the friendship, as Helene did, or discuss the issues at a later date when you've both had time to think things through. At some point you will need to decide whether to stay in the relationship.

Finding Your Authentic Voice

How can Meryl call Jennifer one of her best friends when she lies to her repeatedly? Why does Rebecca still befriend Toby, who gossips behind her back? Confronting a friend or expressing negative feelings in a direct, nonthreatening, nonblaming manner means taking a stand and separating from her. If we look at the merged attachment with our mothers as the model for female friendships, we see that this bond rests on a fusion between two women. The tie allows us to connect intimately and to care for each other in wonderfully responsive ways. Hidden in the warm, fuzzy cocoon we've created, however, lies an excessive concern for others' feelings.[12] We become so worried about hurting another, in fact, that we fear separating (from her) and may even sabotage ourselves.[13]

Growing up, we learn to muffle our authentic voices and become more skillful in protecting the relational "we" than in asserting the autonomous "I."[14] And it's not just that women have difficulty expressing anger or jealousy. *"We avoid asking precise*

questions and making clear statements when we unconsciously sus-
pect that doing so would expose our differences, make the other
person feel uncomfortable, or leave us standing alone," writes Harriet Lerner (her italics).[15]

A recent personal experience brought this point home to me.
Anita, one of my tennis partners, was playing hard, jumping and
slamming volleys, lobbing shots over her opponents' heads, win-
ning point after point for her team. When another of my partners
complimented her on her playing, Anita said, "Don't say that.
You'll make me feel bad." Why would she feel bad for playing
well? Because her superb playing separated her from the rest of
us. She was different, better than the three of us. When Anita
said she feared feeling "bad," she meant she didn't want to feel
guilty for excelling, for leaving us behind. Anita also knew, perhaps unconsciously, that her impressive playing might stir up feelings of envy, anger, and competition in the rest of us.

No one likes to feel bad/guilty. So, to feel good/accepted, we
tone down our opinions, hide our annoyance in a smile. But by
not dealing with our difficulties directly, we remain stuck in the
merged attachment, damage the friendship, or sabotage our own
success. Eichenbaum and Orbach elaborate: "We develop fantasies about what is actually occurring, reading rejection, abandonment and anger when these do not exist. We watch one another
to assess what the other may be feeling rather than articulating
our own feeling or worry. In a sense we remove a part of the self
from the relationship . . . We become distanced from one another
or cut off from parts of ourselves."[16]

Not only does the friendship suffer but we're not able to be
authentic if we must constantly watch ourselves, second-guess
every move, or censor our words. As we've seen again and again,
this is not what we're about at midlife. Yet the alternative—speaking up—can be very frightening if you don't have the tools or the

confidence to carry it off constructively. Or the courage to risk a disconnect.

Speaking Up

About half my sample told me that as they've aged, they've developed the skills to approach a friend when something bothers them. They gained these in various ways: through psychotherapy, assertiveness training, weekend psychological encounters, negotiating in their marriages, or by trial and error. Women who possess the know-how told me that when they first confronted a friend it was definitely frightening. They didn't know how their friend would react or how the encounter would turn out. But they knew their friendship would wither away if they didn't face the issue troubling them. That fact alone motivated them to risk a confrontation.

When I use the word "confrontation," I don't mean a blowout like Emma and Deedee's in *The Turning Point*. I mean an encounter in which you state your concerns or feelings without demeaning or berating your friend, and then hear her out with an open mind. Together you move toward some kind of resolution.

Before you confront a friend, think about all the possible outcomes and whether you can live with the consequences, both positive and negative. Ideally, your honesty will elicit the same from your friend. Your dialogue will draw you closer and your connection will be strengthened. But that doesn't always happen. Your friend may get defensive, back herself into a no-win corner, or refuse to speak to you again. You also need to prepare *yourself* for such a confrontation: You may hear things you don't necessarily want to know.

As we get older, we become less reactive and more thoughtful about confrontations, believes Harriet Lerner. "As we mature, we gain tolerance and perspective. We begin to make more thoughtful decisions about how and when to tell what to whom."

Deciding whether to confront a friend and exactly how to handle the situation depends on your relationship, your history, and your own intuition about the circumstances. Once you decide to risk a confrontation, you might approach another friend for backup support. Discuss your concerns with her or role-play the potential interaction with her. One woman told me that whenever she feels uneasy she runs her feelings by another friend. "This is how I'm feeling," she'll say. "Give me a reality check here."

Don't necessarily expect your husband to encourage you in this area. Several women said that their husbands told them to just forget the issue, that it wasn't that important. One woman said, "When I only used my husband as my sounding board, I didn't get much confidence to confront. I felt like I was this neurotic whiner."

Men don't encourage us to open up difficult issues with a friend, according to Harriet Lerner, because they have less experience talking honestly with male friends. "When they are upset about something, they are more likely to just let it go, and sometimes this works well and sometimes it doesn't. Women have more experience and motivation to try to talk things through. But," she cautions, "women can also overdo that. If trying to talk something through makes it worse, it doesn't help to do more of the same. There are times to just let something go. It's knowing the difference that is the real skill."

Sometimes the hardest part of the encounter is uttering those first few words that initiate the conversation; then the interaction flows by itself. When Dana's father died she called Nikki, a close childhood friend who had moved to London, and left a message with her husband. Nikki didn't call her back. Dana was devastated. After six months she called Nikki again. Dana opened the conversation this way: "I really value our friendship but something has come up that I need to talk about. If I don't, it will fester. I was really hurt that you didn't call when my father died." Nikki apologized and blamed her lapse on the stress of moving abroad. With the air cleared, Dana feels they've recaptured the affection they shared for years.

Dana also now has the strength to speak up when she thinks *she* may have hurt a friend. For an opener, she'll say, "I realize I said such and such the last time we talked. Did I hurt you?" She explains, "I check in on those things rather than hoping nobody will notice. I invite someone to be honest with me." When she thought a colleague seemed indifferent to her, she called her and said, "It seems like things have cooled off between us. I want to be friends. Is everything okay between us?" The colleague was astounded at Dana's perception and reassured her that everything was fine.

A personal experience showed me the importance of speaking up. For about a year every time I talked to Sara, a good friend I've known for twenty-five years, she'd ask, "Are you angry at me?" "No," I insisted. "Everything's fine." We proceeded to chit-chat in summary fashion, not really getting into anything in great depth or sharing much personally. I knew something was deeply wrong but I couldn't tell her. I felt angry, hurt, and abandoned. Sara rarely called me anymore. When I left a message for her, she returned my call a week later. I knew I had invested much more than she had in the friendship and assumed she didn't want to be as close as I did. She seemed satisfied with a superficial phone call every six weeks. I couldn't let her know how much she meant to me. My admission would make me too vulnerable. Besides, I just knew the affection wasn't mutual.

Our friendship continued in this chatty, superficial vein until I ran into her at a party. "What's Margot [my daughter] doing?" Sara asked. Then, "Do you get to the shore much?" These are questions someone would ask who didn't know me very well. I went home in a funk, thinking she wasn't a friend. Even with a twenty-five-year history, we were just acquaintances.

For ten days I debated back and forth whether to tell Sara how I felt. I can't just let the relationship go, I'd think. Yet I couldn't pick up the phone. What am I afraid of? I'd asked myself. Our relationship can't be any worse than it is now, I'd answer. I feared learning the truth: that she wanted to slip out of the friendship and fade out of my life. Yet, in a rational moment, I wondered whether she was reacting to something I did or said. After all, I was making a lot of assumptions about her and how *she* felt.

My husband said, "Let it go. You're just setting yourself up to be hurt again." A close friend just listened and noted how painful it was. Meanwhile I was busy writing this book. From my research I knew that if I didn't speak up, our friendship would die. I gathered my courage and decided to give it one last chance. I had nothing to lose.

I called Sara and asked her to meet me for coffee. When we met I told her I was very upset about our relationship. I said that I felt I had been there for her during a personal crisis. I came over a lot, called often, but after that I felt no appreciation, or any closer connection. I said I felt like I was doing all the calling, that she was not a part of my life, and that my support for her didn't seem to matter. I also acknowledged that she had been there for me during a time of enormous stress.

Sara listened quietly and then said that she felt that I had been angry at her for a long time, but she didn't know why. She felt as though I kept track of whose turn it was to call and that I doled out my feelings in response. If I felt she hadn't called me enough, I withdrew or withheld information from her. After a while, she said, she felt so judged that it became unpleasant talking to me and she stopped calling. Plus, she felt so bad when she got off the phone. "Your friendship was not unconditional," Sara said to me. "It depended on how often I called. I don't feel any different about you whether I talk to you every day or once in two months, but you do."

It disturbed me to learn that I had been so judgmental. I think of myself as an accepting person. But I heard Sara and I also made myself heard: She didn't realize that I needed to touch base frequently. By the end of our discussion, we were both in tears. We told each other how much the friendship meant to us, that we loved each other and wanted to grow old together.

Since that time our friendship has deepened and mellowed. Sara calls or I call: It doesn't matter. We decided to subscribe to a theater series together so we would see each other regularly. In retrospect, I see my judgments as a way of controlling a relationship in which I felt insecure. By letting them go and allowing the friendship to evolve on its own, I freed us both to choose voluntarily whether to stay involved. I now understand that Sara has a vast network of family and friends—far larger than mine—who want pieces of her. I make no demands on her to see me or talk to me. I don't need to—I feel secure in our relationship. I know our caring is mutual and am grateful for and treasure the friendship we have.

Setting Limits

Hard as it is to confront a friend when you feel angry, hurt, or annoyed, it may be more challenging to stand up to a needy friend, precisely *because* she's so needy. It feels like you're hitting her when she's down. But sometimes we must take a stand or set limits when we feel a particular friendship threatens our own integrity or has become unhealthy or toxic for us.

When **Cindy**, a social worker, met Laura on a hike for singles over forty, their problems with men drew them together. They spent hours on the phone at night complaining and commiserating. At first, Cindy griped as much as Laura did, but after a while she grew tired of it and just listened as Laura cried night after night about how her boyfriend mistreated her. Sometimes she'd call at seven-thirty in the morning, sobbing. Cindy felt caught. She dreaded Laura's phone calls. They consumed her evenings and now infringed on her morning time. When she got off the phone, she felt drained and depressed. But she didn't know how to extricate herself from the situation. Besides, she thought, isn't this what friends do for each other?

Out of the blue, an old friend invited Cindy to travel to South America with him. The trip would give her a plan for the leave of absence she had been contemplating and be a perfect antidote to the burnout she felt. Before she left, she made it one of her missions to figure out "why I allow Laura to drive me crazy."

Four months of backpacking and hiking in third-world countries distanced Cindy from her problems. She recalls, "As I'm stomping up this mountain hour after hour, thinking about this, one day I just turned around to my partner and looked at him and said, 'I figured it out!' It just hit me like a bolt of lightning. I realized it was about boundaries. I didn't know that before. When I was so close to it, I kept getting caught up in the emotions."

Cindy realized she had once played the victim in her relationships—the one who got burned, left behind. But not anymore. Laura, however, still immersed herself in that role. When Cindy got home, she confronted her friend. "I've come to a point where I realize I'm responsible for things in my life and I don't want to be the victim, and it's not good for me to hear about it," she told Laura. "Certainly I can be a friend. It's not that I don't want to listen to your problems, but I can't take the constant phone calls or seeing you in the victim role. I love you but you're not helping yourself. I can't watch you do that, and it's not good for me."

She continued, telling Laura, "Our friendship is important. However, this is more important to me. I don't want to end our friendship, but if it means having to relate on that level, then that's what I'll have to do." Laura heard Cindy out, recognized some truth in what she said, and told her she would call less often. She phoned twice a week for a few months and eventually stopped contacting her. When they ran into each other, they chatted briefly.

Cindy told me, "It was a very scary thing for me to confront her. I had never done anything like this in my life—really. All my abandonment issues were coming up, which is funny, because in a way she was driving me crazy, but in another way I didn't want to be rejected and abandoned for who I was," she says. Again, we see how difficult it is to risk a disconnect, an exclusion—even when the person is driving us crazy.

"It was so reaffirming to know I can be who I am," Cindy continues. "I can take that risk to set boundaries. I had no boundaries for a while. I didn't set them with the men I was with, and I learned from her, my women friends. So this was a major step for me to become more my own person and say, 'This is what I will and will not tolerate.' "

Cindy handled the situation tactfully and maturely. She did not accuse Laura but instead used "I" statements, taking full responsibility for her actions. She stated her bottom line: "I cannot listen to you talk about being in the victim role. It's not good for me." She was willing to walk away from the friendship if necessary. The friendship eventually ended because they lost their common ground.

That confrontation gave Cindy the confidence she needed to stand up for herself. Today she uses it as a model when she runs into trouble in her other relationships, male and female. She says, "I'm more willing to take that risk to say what's really going on with me. I still worry that I'm going to hurt someone's feelings, so I need to keep working on it. But I'm getting much better at stating my needs."

Setting limits with a friend or speaking up when we feel angry, hurt, or jealous does get easier each time we do it. With every success, our confidence grows. Instead of sacrificing ourselves or compromising our friendships, we can all develop the skills, as Cindy did, to stand up for issues that matter to us. Consider these challenging situations as opportunities to expand your repertoire of relating and strengthen your connections to friends.

Chapter Four

Married with Friends

"The truth is, friendship is to me every bit as sacred and eternal as marriage."

Katherine Mansfield

We zoom down I-95 headed to a friend's wedding in Baltimore. Dick and I, newlyweds, hold hands in the backseat. My friend Linda, seated next to her husband Joe, cranes her neck to talk to me as he navigates the weekend traffic. "Isn't he weaving too much?" Dick whispers to me. "Where'd he learn to drive?" I shush him and go back to my conversation with Linda. Occasionally Dick asks Joe a question or makes a comment, but mostly the guys fade into the background. Our foursome centers on Linda's and my friendship.

Two years later Dick and I were living in the suburbs and I lost touch with Linda and my other center-city friends who were still working full-time and childless. By now, I had a six-month-old baby and a part-time social-work job. On my days off, I'd walk Andrew to the park, desperate to meet another mom. For months I never stumbled on a soul. Then I met a woman pushing her daughter on the swings who invited me to join a play group with three other mothers from the neighborhood. The following year I participated in a baby-sitting co-op, then a women's support group, and a couple of years after that we joined a synagogue. There I met the women who became my good friends. We commiserated as working mothers, celebrated holidays together with our families, and went out as couples.

In retrospect, I realize that while raising my family I spent very little time alone with friends. My social life centered on my volunteer activities at the synagogue and the children's schools. I hardly remember ever meeting a friend for lunch. Most of my real connecting occurred during my early-morning fast-walks with two close friends whom I've met on alternate days for over fifteen years. Between baseball practice and gymnastic lessons, religious-school car pools, obligations with in-laws, running a home, and building a new career as a freelance writer, I had little time to spare. I knew my friends and I cared about each other and would be available in a crisis, but for all of us, our husbands and children came first.

Those active, family-centered years flew by. Before I knew it Andrew and Margot had left for college. Almost instantly, friends became more important to me and more integral to my life. Not only did I have more time for friends, but they filled a deep, urgent need. But when I look back, I wonder: Did I really *not* care whether I saw so little of my friends early on? How did I let my social-work buddies slip away so easily? Perhaps Dick sent subtle messages that he should be my primary and only concern. I vaguely remember a couple of times when he ridiculed the husband of a friend, although I can't recall any particular comments. Yet he didn't make me feel guilty when I went out, nor did he criticize my friends, as some husbands did. But then again, my friends did not consume huge chunks of my time or energy, so he had no reason to. Still, I sensed he had some difficulty sharing me with others.

"Marriage is one of the biggest of life's *friendshifts*," says sociologist Jan Yager, Ph.D., who coined the term "friendshifts" to signify how our friendships change as we move from one stage of life to another.[1] If you're married, you know that a complex relationship exists between marriage and friendship. Not only do our husbands affect our friendships but they, in turn, impact on our marriages. At midlife do our husbands still see our friends as a competing source of intimacy and loyalty? And if so, how do we handle those concerns now? To shed light on our husbands' perspective, it helps to understand male development at midlife. Our husbands may not realize, however, that far from sabotaging a marriage, friends can complement and stabilize it, promote fidelity, and enhance a woman's self-esteem.

Sharing the Wealth

As I interviewed women for this book, I learned that my friendship-and-marriage history was far from unique. Many women told me similar stories of how their pals faded into the background while they raised their families. Several studies have also shown that time spent with friends decreases during periods of heavy family responsibility.[2] I did not have a best friend during those years. Women who did had to contend with their husbands' jealousy over the time and energy that relationship robbed from the family. "He hated her," one woman said, speaking of her husband and best friend. "Every time she called, he'd say, 'That bitch is on the phone.' Or if we had a fight, he'd say, 'Now you won't be friends, right?' He just couldn't get it."

Why can't our husbands get it? Or do they now, after all these years? Of the twenty-nine married women in my sample, twenty-four described their husbands' reactions to their friends in positive terms. The responses ranged from "tolerant" to "accepting" to "supportive" to "encouraging" their wives to see their friends. Several said their husbands "relish" their friends today, because the men recognize how vital friends are to their wives' happiness. Another said her husband saw her friends as enriching *his* life as well as hers. How ironic that men respond so positively to their wives' friends at midlife when in fact, women's friendships run deeper, play a more central role in their lives, and command more of their time than ever before.

Clearly, most men have mellowed in terms of accepting the presence and importance of friends to their wives. Only five, or one out of six married women in my sample, complained that their husbands still harbor resentments and jealousy. **Meryl**, who has been married for twenty-six years to Neal, says when they dated, he marveled that she seemed to know everyone on campus. But once they got married, her sociability became a bone of contention. Every time she wanted to go out, he'd grill her, asking: "Why do you have to go to Gourmet Club?" "Why can't you stay home?" "Why do you have to be out another night?"

Gradually, he accepted that she liked a lot of people in her life. "I get a kick out of people, talking to strangers or forging friendships," she said. "Just put me in a pool with water and I can swim. It's just something that happens. I put other people at ease and I have fun. It's no big deal for me. It's just an adventure. It's cool to find out people's stories."

Neal, much shier and more restrained, takes longer to warm up to people. Even those who know him well find him hard to read. His fantasy of a perfect evening? Having Meryl sit quietly beside him on the sofa with an open book on her lap.

After years of bickering, Meryl believes they have found ways to accommodate and accept each other. Following a trial separation, they bought a condo at the beach, where they spend weekends alone. No friends and no phones. She also takes no telephone calls when Neal is home. If she's talking on the phone and he walks in, she'll hang up immediately, saying, "Neal's here. Bye." Her friends know not to call her in the evening.

We all make accommodations in marriage, some larger than others. Meryl explains her rationale. "We used to fight about my friends, but now I think he's right. In this world, we have so few hours together. He'd say, 'You have all day every day. You can do whatever you want, go wherever you want.'" She paused. "He's right. 'Do what you want during the day, but when night-time comes and we're together, it's a sacred thing. We should really cherish that.' He says that and I actually believe that. I fought it for a long time, but now I think it's really nice. Having a good relationship with a spouse is really the ultimate friendship."

It sounds as though Meryl is trying to convince herself that Neal knows what's best for her. The question is not whether seeing her friends and talking to them during the day is enough, but whether that is her choice. For another woman, Neal's stipulations would feel suffocating. Only Meryl knows the extent to which her marriage satisfies or stifles her personal needs.

Why do men like Neal have such a hard time sharing their wives with their friends? According to psychotherapists and coauthors Luise Eichenbaum and Susie Orbach, no matter how loving and caring a husband may be, he still has tremendous difficulty with "the autonomy and separateness" of his wife. A man *appears* more independent only because his dependency needs are more constantly satisfied, first by his mother, then by his girlfriend and wife. The man threatened by his wife's separateness feels abandoned and lonely when she's not around. He may feel inadequate, too: If he were enough, she wouldn't need others.[3] Of course, he's not in touch with these feelings. He only knows he feels uneasy when she's not there and blames her friends for taking her away from him.

Culturally, however, we cannot entirely blame men for wanting us all to themselves. Since the beginning of the nineteenth century, sociologists have touted the pie-in-the-sky notion of the "companionate marriage"—a union in which our husbands become our best and only friends as well as our lovers. Based on the "fund of sociability" theory, this model suggests that everyone requires a certain level of intimate experiences, and if marriage provides these, we don't need any other relationships.[4] No doubt, women questioned this theory privately for years, but it took the women's movement to give them permission to share the intimacies of their lives and find acceptance for speaking out about how much their friends meant to them.

Women's Ways

Women yearn for satisfying marriages *and* good friendships. We love our husbands, but . . . They're not enough. Especially now. With the kids gone, our parents ailing or dying, our husbands aging, and our marriages experiencing midlife transitions, we need friends to fill the holes in our hearts. Friends and husbands serve different purposes, fill different needs, respond differently. They are not mutually exclusive.

According to a British study of sixty married women, a woman with a close friend is just as likely to confide in her husband as someone without a close friend.[5] Revealing secrets to a spouse, however, does not necessarily mean that he's supportive—paradoxical as this seems. Living with a man fosters sharing simply because he's available, yet that does not automatically translate into his encouraging his wife's development,[6] particularly in personal or professional areas that could make her more independent.

It is our friends who encourage us to stretch and strive, whether it involves returning to school, buying a franchise, splurging for a spiritual retreat, or accepting an invitation to give a keynote address. "I talk to friends about my frustrations being married to someone who is content and would like to retire and play golf," a forty-nine-year-old teacher who has been married for thirty years told me. "I don't know *when* I'm going to retire or *if* I'm going to retire. I want to constantly change and grow. When I talk to him about that, it becomes an area of conflict. He wants me to be the woman I was who would meet him at the front door and hang up his clothes. I don't do that anymore."

The British study revealed only one aspect of the marital relationship that related to confiding in a friend: Those who did not feel financially secure did not attempt to form or maintain friendships.[7] Additional research also found working-class women less likely to have close friends than those from the middle class, perhaps because the former must concern themselves with subsistence issues and have less leisure time. They also tend to live closer to family and interact more often with relatives.

Woman after woman told me how her friends understand her anxieties while her husband insists on offering a solution or fixing the problem at hand. The following comment is typical. "Friends are more accepting of me than my husband," one woman said. "I can say to a friend a thousand times, 'I'm so fat, I want chocolate.' If I say that to my husband, he'll say, 'Why don't you do something about it?' He harangues me while they lament with me."

Friends know how to "be there" during a crisis, while husbands have difficulty hearing our pain, perhaps because they can't remedy it. One woman, on the verge of divorce after twenty-five years of marriage, spoke of how her husband disappointed her after the death of her father. "I expected my husband to be there, but he just could not rise to the occasion. For a while I thought it was because his own father was still alive, but his father died three months later and he just did that stoic thing, like, 'Oh, I can walk through everything.' It was a very difficult experience for me." Her comments reflect more than a wish for a more supportive husband. They show her deep disillusionment with him as a person. She goes on: "It was my girlfriends who supported me and propped me up so I could stand on my own. They called, sent cards, wrote notes. They just came and sat with me . . . whatever I needed."

When frightened, we can talk about real fear with a friend, whereas we tend to protect our husbands. If you share with your husband your worries about your daughter driving across the country, you'll have to cope with his fears and anxieties as well as your own. Because a friend invests in your family differently than a spouse, she can be there for you without wallowing in the emotion *with* you, as a husband might.

"You can say to a friend, 'I'm terrified.' You can say it to a husband, too, but you're always worried about what your fear will do to him," insists Helen, speaking of her own thirty-year marriage. "You're always trying not to let too much out. With a friend you don't have to worry about that. It's not that we don't care about how much we load on each other. When you're in a crisis, a friend can take it. If she can't, she simply won't be there. It's that clean."

Women do couch their fears with their husbands, but why? "They know that husbands often don't handle fears very well, and they do protect them, especially around physical illness," says psychiatrist Jean Baker Miller. "Say a woman gets a breast lump. Her husband will do things that look terrible, like not pick her up from the doctor when she needs a ride. It looks so cruel, but I have realized it's because he's so afraid."

Jean Baker Miller believes men become frightened when their wives appear vulnerable. Not knowing how to handle their feelings in an open way, men avoid them altogether. Women know that about their husbands and intuitively protect them. "They sense that men are frightened and not good at handling their fears. Many women are still trained to emotionally protect the men they care about. I do think that's true," Dr. Miller notes, adding, "Women know that with all the bluster, men really are boys underneath and you have to take care of them. It's a funny thing: Women do that and yet at the same time there's this impression that men are the strong ones."

Mix and Match

Women blend their husbands and friends into a savory potpourri, mixing and merging them to suit their needs. Many a woman calls her husband her best friend, but that does not preclude her also claiming a female best friend and other close chums. When a woman gives her husband that designation, she often bases it on history and familiarity. With a female friend, the label signifies the intimacy they share.

Marissa, fifty, calls Ava, her business partner in their marketing firm, her best friend. But so is Joel, her husband of twenty years. "We've been through so much together that Joel is definitely my best friend. But I confide more in Ava than I do in him. We have almost more allegiance to each other, more secrets *from* our husbands than we do *with* our husbands. Nothing indiscreet about anybody cheating or having an affair. Mostly financial stuff," she says.

"Joel doesn't take an interest in a lot of things that I confide in other people. The more we're together, the more we speak in shorthand. We communicate better but more briefly, too," she says with a laugh.

Marissa confides a lot of gossipy things to Ava, especially about her eleven-year-old daughter's social life. "Joel's a little over-zealous in that area—no this, no that, no boys. It's all very innocent, but rather than get him stirred up . . ." Her voice trails off.

She continues to contrast her two best friends. "I pick my spots with Joel—when I tell him, what I tell him, how I tell him. We're not talking about big things. Big things I would just tell. It's all those little day-to-day incidents that I know would get a big reaction when I'm not in the mood for a big reaction, so I just save. At another point it may come up. It may not. It may just go by the wayside, and he would never know."

Whether women have a best buddy or an inner circle of friends, it is their connection to one another that gratifies their deep emotional needs—not a Saturday-night gourmet meal or a movie and pizza with another couple. That's fun and entertaining but usually superficial, even with a close friend and her spouse.

Many women told me they have couple friends distinct from their women friends. Some couples rarely go out with others, either because the husband wants his wife to himself or they can't find couples they both like. Some wives would like this to change; others don't care because they make sure they satisfy their emotional needs elsewhere. At this stage of life, married women also have a number of single, divorced, and widowed friends whom they usually see alone, rather than accompanied by their husbands.

Most married women have their own social lives with friends during the week; they may also meet a friend on a Saturday for lunch or shopping. But they consider Friday and Saturday evening "date night," and go out with their spouses alone or with another couple. With this arrangement, they can meet their own needs as well as their husbands'. Connie and John, both teachers, have been married for twenty-eight years. When their sons were in high school, she decided to go to graduate school for social work. Up until that time her friendships revolved around the children's activities in school and sports. She socialized only as part of a couple.

Going back to school altered, not only the time she could devote to friendships, but, she said, "I wanted deeper connections. It wasn't just home and school or shuttling the children back and forth. It was more directed and filling a need that I had. That felt more honest. My time became very limited. I was working full-time and going to school at night, and as I learned more about myself, I was able to put something different into my friendships."

Consequently, she says, "New friendships developed, because I became freer and was able to identify what my needs were as opposed to what *our* needs were as a couple. For many years I considered my husband my best friend. But as I altered my life, he became not my *only* best friend. No, I'm not divorced," she quickly adds.

In the first twenty years of her marriage, Connie devoted all her attention to John. If he didn't like a friend or her husband, she would drop them. "I went along," she admits. "If it didn't work as a couple, it didn't become part of my life. I allowed some of those friendships to slip away. In retrospect, I think, I missed something there."

Today Connie has three close women friends whom she fast-walks with before work or meets for lunch or dinner during the week. She and John rarely go out with another couple on the weekend, because he prefers to be alone with her. Connie complies with his wishes, even though she's not entirely pleased with their social life. The arrangement helps ease her guilt for spending so much time away from John during the week.

On a Collision Course?

Within the last few years Dick dug up part of the backyard to plant a vegetable garden, took up the recorder, and began tinkering in the kitchen. He is not unique. As men's need to prove themselves subsides at midlife, they become less focused on success and achievement and more interested in exploring their softer, creative sides and nurturing their relationships. After completing a seven-year study, including five hundred personal interviews, for her book *New Passages,* Gail Sheehy found that "the important shift for men in middle life is from competing to connecting."[8] Connecting to music and the arts, to nature, to spirituality, to their emotions, and to their wives and children.

Not all men welcome this passage with open arms, however. Some have difficulty accepting their more "feminine" side and feel that such tender, emotional, and aesthetic qualities are unworthy of a "real man." They attempt to recapture their masculinity through alcohol, affairs with younger women, or by dominating their wives.[9] You could say that these men don't make the passage to the next phase of their lives.

Those of us married to sensitive men, however, have finally gained what we've always wanted: someone who will listen to us and share his emotions. But here's the rub: It takes an unusual man, after over twenty-five years of stoic nonresponsiveness, to suddenly reveal his innermost feelings. To compound the problem, while he winds down professionally, we're revving up on all cylinders. We've landed the graduate degree, or opened our own business, or are committed to fighting illiteracy. With parenting responsibilities behind us, we feel energetic, motivated, and purposeful. This can be intimidating to a man who feels vulnerable personally and superfluous and ineffectual at work as he watches young turks move up and take over. He fears losing his youth and sex appeal. Most likely he has gained a few pounds around his middle, is losing his hair, suffers bouts of impotence, and gets out of breath after a game of tennis.

He turns to his family for comfort. But where are they now? Slowly he begins to grasp how he missed years of his children's lives by working long hours, or he remembers the nights he came home preoccupied with work problems and could not "be there" for his family. Just as he's ready to reach out to his children as young adults, they leave home. Regrets engulf him.

When our children depart, we're left home alone with our husbands. No more distractions. No excuses. No escape hatch. Inevitably, unresolved issues, buried for years, reemerge—only we see them through eyes that have weathered years of marriage. One woman, who suspected for years that her husband might be an alcoholic, finally confronted him and owned up to her part in their battles. When he came home drunk in the past, she'd harangue him and they'd fight until three A.M. Now she realized that she had remained in the marriage for the kids and had no reason to stay any longer. When he came home drunk recently, she told him, "I'm here because I want to be here. I'm sick of arguing." And she went to bed. She is determined not to fight about his binges anymore. If he continues drinking, she is prepared to leave.

New concerns surface as we cope with the psychological repercussions of our own aging as well as our husbands'. Where did the passion go? How bad is this health scare? Is retirement right for you? Some marriages self-destruct without children, while others seize these issues to mine deeper levels of intimacy.

A disconcerting study by Margaret Fiske Lowenthal and

Lawrence Weiss, done while they were professors in the Human
Development Program at the University of California at San Francisco, found that eighteen months after the youngest child left
home, husbands and wives experienced similar high levels of har-
mony and happiness, almost like a second honeymoon. But five
years later the researchers found the long-range goals of husbands
and wives on a collision course. Many women hoped to commit
themselves to an activity or interest beyond the family, while their
husbands wanted more pampering from their wives to ease them
through the next ten or fifteen years of boredom on their jobs[10]—
almost as though the husband filled the hole in the family by
becoming the child who left.

Thus, our husbands become more reliant on us just as we begin
to savor our freedom after launching our children and encouraging *their* independence. In interviews for her two most recent
books, *New Passages* and *Understanding Men's Passages,* Gail
Sheehy found that all the professional men over fifty whom she
interviewed named their wives as their primary source of intimacy
and comfort. Every single one.[11] Of midlife men, Sheehy writes,
"Wary of allowing other men to glimpse any cracks in the armor
or sores on the soul, [they] tend to raise their guard even higher
than before. They rarely make new friends. They may become
emotionally dependent on their wives, even dangerously so."[12] In
my interviews as well, the majority of married women told me
that their husbands considered them their best and, often, only
real friend.

Whether we consider our husbands our best friends or one of
several people we feel close to, we need not continue on a collision
course with them. Midlife can be a wonderful stage for a couple
if we can abandon our outdated, stereotypical roles and expand
our visions of each other. Our husbands should not count on us
to coddle them or put our needs second to theirs. We need to

appreciate the ways in which their lives are changing and the difficulty these adjustments present for them. Together, we can revitalize our marriages by bringing our individual interests home, introducing new people to each other, exploring different hobbies, and reviving old interests as a couple.

Dick and I have played tennis for years. He plays with a group of men and I with a group of women. We play together occasionally in the summer or when we're on vacation, but tennis has never been a big part of our social life. Last summer we started playing tennis on Sunday mornings with Bill, a college friend of Dick's, and his wife Nancy. We've known them for years, attend each other's life-cycle events, and go out as couples about twice a year. Dick and Bill talk frequently. Since we've started playing tennis regularly through the summer and fall, Nancy and I have begun sharing more and more of our lives. I've developed a new appreciation and affection for both of them. Talking over brunch just last week, we all agreed that our Sunday-morning date ranked as one of the highlights of our week.

The Gifts of Friendship

Ironically, friends can play an important role in keeping our marriages intact and alive. Not only do friends meet needs that our husbands can't, but friends provide a safe haven that allows us to "process" the dynamics of our marriages. With close friends, we can let off steam, think aloud, and reassess our perceptions and pet peeves. Our friends also help us plan communication with our spouses, generate compassion or appreciation for them, and effect changes in our own attitudes and behavior.[13]

In all these ways, our interactions with friends accommodate and protect our marriages. As long as we're married, we reinforce each other's commitment to the union. Rarely do we bad-mouth a friend's husband, no matter how negatively she may talk. Once the divorce becomes final, *then* we can tell her how we really feel about her ex-husband.

If a friend believes marriage is in our best interest, she may remind us of a husband's attributes or even point out that we would be sorry or wrong to leave. When Tina's friend heard she had an appointment with a divorce attorney, she deliberately intercepted her and invited her to lunch before the meeting. "You're just going on raw emotion," she told Tina. "You need to talk this through. You're going to go in there and tell your tale to a professional whose business is to get your business. He's not going to talk you out of this." After lunch, Tina canceled her appointment with the lawyer and went home to talk to her husband. They're still together.

Not all situations end quite so dramatically. But friends can provide a safety valve for our emotions and an objective perspective when we're steeped in rage or frustration. Helen, who married at nineteen and had three children in close succession, completed her college education in the last five years. Midway through her courses, she asked Sam, her husband of thirty years, to critique an important paper. "That was stupid on my part because he really had no feel for the subject matter," she says. "He critiqued it okay, but it just hit such a bad chord with me that I blew up." She blasted him for not supporting her and marched off to the library in a huff. As she stared blankly at the string of words on the page, she created scenarios about how Sam would sabotage her future and what her life would be like without him.

She shared her worst-case fantasies with Terri, a very good friend, who just listened. A week later she called Helen back and asked, "How do you feel about Sam, school, and the paper? Are you still thinking of splitting?" Helen said she got busy on the next paper and forgot about it. "Good," Terri said, "because you really were off-the-wall." As they talked, Helen realized that she still harbored a lot of anger, because she had dropped out of college to marry Sam. Even though she was a willing and eager participant in her youthful marriage, unconsciously she held Sam responsible for interrupting her education. By talking with Terri, Helen realized that returning to school had revived resentment that lay dormant for almost thirty years.

While our friends support *us* and our commitment to marriage, they may show it by offering a husband's viewpoint, which in turn, can make us more understanding and patient with him. When Kathryn's husband Mac took early retirement, she had a difficult time adjusting to his presence around the house, because she worked at home. She recalls, "I used my friendships to vent quite a bit during that time. If I hadn't had them, our situation would have been much more explosive. Not only did they support me but they were pretty clear-eyed about what was going on," she remembers. "I wanted them to be one hundred percent behind me and see my point of view, and yet they told me the hard truth: Mac is having adjustment problems, too. They helped me understand his point of view, which I couldn't hear from him. When he told me, I got very defensive."

Our friends also help us appreciate our husbands' strengths rather than dwelling on their frailties. Maybe he bungles projects around the house; a good friend will remind you of how he's willing to get estimates and negotiate with workmen about a construction project. Annoying personal habits can seem petty when you relate them to a friend, who reminds you of the surprise party he planned for your birthday or the way he picked up the slack at home when you had to work overtime. Talking with friends about our husbands' limitations helps us accept them and view our marriages more realistically. At this point we no longer harbor illusions of being married to a perfect man, but when we're furious or perturbed we tend to discount "the big picture" and obsess on the negatives.

After being married for years, we know whether our husbands will listen one more time to our frustrations with a boss or our resentment at a sister or brother. We don't have to go through the process of reporting an incident and then feeling angry that they spaced out or launched into their own problems during a pause in our story. Now we proceed directly to a friend, who provides a willing and sympathetic ear.

By being there, listening and accepting us during the rough patches, our friends actually reinforce our marriages. Maureen learned this about five years ago when her husband experienced a deep depression after his diagnosis of congestive heart failure. He withdrew completely from her. "The fact that I could get together with my friends and share my feelings of despair—I was missing the man that I had married—gave me the strength to go back and cope at home. It gave me more energy," she says. "It didn't solve the problems, but at least I felt as if I had a voice there."

Every time **Marissa**'s marriage has been tested, her best friend Ava has been her biggest confidante and booster. Recently she couldn't sleep following a heated argument with Joel. The next day, "Ava listened, she repeated back what I said and did not judge me," Marissa recalls. "She told me about how her marriage had been tested, how she thinks of leaving but always decides against it. Miserable as she is, she'll pretend to be happy, but then six months later she doesn't know if she's pretending or it's real," Marissa says, laughing. "She also encourages me to take baby steps. I tend to look for the big cure."

Our friendships also bolster us so we can face our marriages more affirmed in who we are as women, not just as wives. We need that more than our husbands do, because marriage doesn't strip men so profoundly of their personal identity.[14] Most of us took our husbands' names, submerged our professional goals to further theirs. Although these patterns are changing in our daughters' generation, many of us still need our friends' encouragement to assert ourselves so we don't lose our own identities in the "we" of marriage.

When Marissa first met Ava, she and Joel had never spent twenty-four hours apart. They worked together at an ad agency and lived together. "He was very jealous early on," Marissa says. "I definitely needed permission to do just about anything separate from him. I had cut off a lot of friendships because of him. Ava made me rethink a lot of that. She gave me an ally. It wasn't just me anymore. It was me and Ava. She encouraged me to get away. Once Ava and I became business partners we would travel together. She helped me distance myself a little bit and find ways of not putting everything in my marriage. That friendship has definitely given my life a better balance."

Over the years, Marissa says, her friendship with Ava has provided a refuge in which she received permission to talk about her marriage and gave her courage to act when necessary. "Our discussions allowed me to work out issues so I could go back to Joel and confront him," she says. "Talking about my marriage and husband had always been taboo. But I could do that in this friendship."

Only two of the married women in my sample did not discuss their marriages or marital problems with friends. One believed her five years of psychotherapy had taught her how to communicate with her husband, so she didn't need her friends as a sounding board. Martha, a practical, no-nonsense woman who tends to keep her own counsel, presented another point of view. She told me, "I don't like to create bad energy. I don't talk about my kids, either. I'm very reluctant to tell negative things, because I believe in the good energy coming out. If a friend has told me terrible things about her husband, it changes my relationship to both of them."

In addition, Martha says, "I'm very unlikely to complain. It doesn't seem to do anything. I'd rather tell *him,* not them [her friends]. I usually hate it when I've done it—like I've polluted something. Plus, there's not a lot to complain about, so it seems so small, whatever I might happen to say. I just feel like it would be a betrayal." While Martha's perspective is certainly valid for her, the majority of women in my study, particularly those married more than twenty years, do not see talking to their friends as a betrayal of their marriages.

Liberating Liaisons

Research studies increasingly confirm that married women's friendships make a significant contribution to their well-being.[15] One showed that when married women had one or more close, mutual friendships, they were significantly less depressed, more satisfied with their lives, and had higher self-esteem than those without such connections.[16] Another study cited friendship as an independent source of happiness over and above marriage and family, and found that for some, friends mattered more than husbands.[17] One woman I interviewed put it this way: "I feel guilty saying this, but if somebody said you couldn't have your girlfriends *and* your husband, I think I'd give up my husband and keep my girlfriends. They mean that much to me. He's the kindest man going, but they fill more of an emotional need for me than he does."

No one else expressed that conviction quite so boldly, but

many married women suggested that they preferred the company of their friends to their husbands. A forty-nine-year-old interior designer told me, "I just love my girlfriends. I would rather take a vacation with them. We have the best time. We have so much fun that we embarrass our children sometimes." Another, who just celebrated her twenty-fifth anniversary, said, "I'm at a point in my life where I find my female friends infinitely more interesting. The men are okay but once is enough."

Friendships can be liberating at this stage. "They give you a forum that you don't have with any of your other hats on. You can be as young or old as you want to be, as irresponsible as you wish. That's what my friendship with Ava is about," Marissa muses. "We laugh so much. We can be very irreverent and say the wildest things that would scare our husbands and children to death."

Marissa often teases her friends that she's going to chuck all her obligations and hop the next plane to Paris. "It's just a joke," she says. "I'm not acting on it, but Joel would not like to hear that." Being able to share her fantasies about abandoning her responsibilities helps her cope with her frustrations as she juggles her roles as wife, mother, and marketing consultant. She's not going to break loose but being able to talk about her yearning makes staying more tolerable and infinitely sweeter. Summing up how many married women feel, Marissa says, "My friendships are very much a catharsis."

Chapter Five

Alone but Not Lonely

"Nobody, but nobody
Can make it out here alone."

Maya Angelou

When Christine, a fifty-one-year-old nurse, had been married for fifteen years she learned that her husband was gay. Shocked and ashamed, she also became strangely protective of him. To remain loyal to her marriage, she felt she must not say a word to anyone about their predicament. "I felt that if the marriage was going to have a chance, it couldn't be talked about, that talking about it would end it." She laughs now at her crazy reasoning.

"There was no place to turn. There wasn't a soul I could think of to talk to, because I wanted the marriage to last," she continues. "So I didn't talk to my friends. It was the loneliest period of my life. I've always been a very outgoing person. I wasn't used to keeping secrets and here was the biggest one and I had nowhere to put it."

When she separated from her husband three years later, Christine still did not discuss the reasons with anyone. Only when the divorce became final did she confide in three women, carefully selected from her acquaintances, because she considered them compassionate and trustworthy. She had always liked Marcia, the mother of her daughter's best friend, who lived in her neighborhood. "Marcia and her husband David saved my life. Emotionally—they certainly did," she recalls. "They told me to call at three A.M. if I couldn't sleep. They invited me to every single family event, and if Marcia couldn't go someplace, David would ask me, which I thought was very loving of both of them."

Christine told another longtime friend who lived across the country because she knew her secret would be safe with her. But no one at work knew of her circumstances. One day while eating lunch in the cafeteria with a group of nurses from her floor, she mentioned that she was newly divorced. Later that day a nurse, who had just joined the staff, passed her a note that read, "I'm on my own, too. If you want to go for a movie, give me a call." Christine recalls, "That was the friendliest gesture when I really needed a friendly gesture."

The year her divorce became final, two other significant events nearly felled her: Her son left for college and her mother died. "I felt I was no longer a mother, a daughter, or a wife all at once," Christine says. "Without those dear friends, I would have really been lost." Seven years later these three women—one married and two divorced—have become Christine's closest friends. Like other divorced, widowed, and never-married women, Christine has learned that you don't have to be married to feel supported, that you can satisfy your intimacy needs in a variety of ways and create a sense of community and connection without a traditional family. Among those connections, female friendships stand out.

Revising the Dream

For much of the twentieth century, being single carried a stigma. The cultural messages, both overtly and covertly, implied that marriage must be every woman's dream, that the traditional family offered the best chance of happiness, and that only by bearing children could a woman fulfill her destiny.[1] Society valued a woman only when she was attached to a man—not for who she was as a person.

While these views are changing, the remnants of the old messages still affect single women today, particularly those over forty. Do you still hear the voice of your mother or grandmother reminding you: "Don't eat the last piece of cake or you'll be an old maid." Heaven forbid! Or, "The way to a man's heart is through his stomach"—implying that you must do whatever you need to do—even cook—to catch a man so you won't be alone. Although mothers convey their messages more subtly to their grown daughters today, they still take their toll. When Christine divorced after her husband came out, her mother berated her for causing the divorce and urged her to stay married anyhow. To her mother, marriage—under any circumstance—was preferable to being single.

On the other hand, Cindy, a forty-seven-year-old social worker in the adoption field, says, "If I got any message from my mother, it's that you don't need a man. She was always so self-sufficient and independent. (My father died thirty years ago.) I'm very grateful for that message, but I still feel sort of ashamed. I'm not married. I don't have kids. Am I good enough—as far as in this society?" she questions. Her best friend has never married either; her four other closest friends are either single or divorced. Sharing her feelings of inadequacy with her single friends helps Cindy feel less defective. They validate her lifestyle and her choices. After all, she figures, we're in the same boat. We can't *all* be bad. Because some of her unmarried friends do have children, she has also raised these issues with single male friends and was surprised to find that they, too, share similar sentiments.

For women, however, the fear of not measuring up, of not being good enough, stems—again—from the romantic vision most of us grew up with: that we would fall in love, marry Prince Charming, and live happily ever after. As a young girl, who among us dreamed of becoming a powerful attorney or a CEO? Even if divorce or death forces a woman to abandon part of the dream— the man—she often feels guilty for disappointing her family,[2] as Christine did.

A 1997 study of seventy-eight single women at midlife by Karen Gail Lewis, a family therapist, and Sidney Moon, an educational psychologist, found that women know the advantages of being single—the freedom from taking care of a man, the ability to do what they want when they want and how they want; and not having to answer to others for their time, decisions, and behaviors. They also recognize the drawbacks—the absence of touch, of children, and of being special to a man, the lack of ready companionship, and sadness about growing old alone.[3] The women told the researchers that although they feel basically content being single, they also experience feelings of loss and grief. Much of their ambivalence stems from self-blame. All the women in the study criticized themselves for being single.[4] No wonder single women have mixed feelings about their status.

But is a single woman's ambivalence any different from the complex feelings a married woman has about being married? Probably not. Except that a married woman can voluntarily change her status. A single woman has control over *looking* for a partner but not over *finding* one.[5] To a single woman, married life can appear very cozy and easy, although anyone who has been married knows that marriage requires work and has many difficult moments.

Just as married women commiserate about coupled life with their married friends, so single women find solace and solidarity in sharing their concerns with other singles. Particularly as they get older. "Friends are my safety net, my security net, my family," said a divorced director of community programs. "I don't have to age alone." Certainly, the support of good friends helps single women accept themselves and their situation.

But they need something else as well, say psychologists Carol M. Anderson and Susan Stewart, who studied ninety successful single women between the ages of forty and fifty-five. In order to lead rich, satisfying lives, single women need to abandon the dream, so they can move on. *"Giving up The Dream is not acceptance of deprivation but rather an affirmation of self,"* say the researchers. At some point every woman in their study decided to stop waiting for her prince and took charge of her own life. This process creates sadness initially, because women must grieve for the roles of wife and mother that they will never know. Once they come to terms with these losses, though, a new sense of freedom awaits them and an enormous range of possibilities unfolds.[6]

Birds of a Feather

A special connection exists among single women, whether they were married at one time or have always been single. At midlife they share a similar lifestyle; usually they live alone. They all cope with the challenges of loneliness, isolation, and fear of the future as well as the rewards of freedom, solitude, and close friendships. "There's definitely a bonding among single people, because we realize that in our lifetime we need each other a lot, especially as we're getting older," Cindy says. "We tend to have this sort of silent unspoken bond that hey, we don't have a family other than our family of origin, and so we need to look out for each other." When Cindy had knee surgery, her friends drove her to the hospital, filled her prescriptions at the drugstore, and cooked her dinners for a week. With every encounter, they checked in to see how she was doing emotionally.

Another woman, divorced for a decade, said to me, "I see myself being more serious about friendships than ten years ago. I'm more willing to make clear what I'm looking for and what I need and want, so my friendships last. I take them as seriously as I took relationships with men and depend on friends in a way I thought only a heterosexual relationship would serve me." She lists her best friend's name and telephone number on the emergency card in her wallet.

"We really are like sisters," says Karen, forty-nine, speaking of her tight circle of friends. She divorced fifteen years ago after a brief marriage. "We have history—a twenty-year history. We see each other at our absolute worst and at our absolute best. We've been there for each other in a way that our families haven't. Five years ago I had a hysterectomy. One of my friends who knows my relationship with my family came in to my hospital room and said—she didn't ask—'You won't go to your mother's. You won't go to your sister's. You'll come to my house.' That was that. So for six weeks of her life—and I was not in good shape after surgery—she coddled me and made my life heaven. That's a friend. An incredible friend."

Karen sees her family at showers, births, weddings, and funerals, but her friends provide daily support. "It's not unusual for one of us in this group of women to call another out of the blue and say, 'You're not going to believe what happened to me.' We know the minutiae of each other's lives. We sort of live day-today with each other. I make it sound like we talk every day. Sometimes we do, and sometimes we don't talk for weeks. Yet there is still that closeness."

Closeness also comes from venturing together into uncharted territory. "There's no template for single women, as there is for the married woman with children. We're feeling our way. We're not sure. There aren't a lot of rules for us," Cindy laments, noting a special bond among women who never married or had children. Married and divorced women with children can mark developmental milestones for their children and themselves as they proceed from pregnancy and birth to launching their children into the world. Childless women who never married lack these demarcations and the gratifications that accompany them. They can take pride in their careers, although, for some, that may not bring the same emotional rewards.

Contending with a New Status

If you become widowed or divorced at midlife, friends are invaluable. Say you've endured a long illness with a spouse or gone through a painful divorce. No doubt your close friends ministered to you day after day. But without a husband, your status has changed. And so might your friends.

Sue dropped Mary, her closest friend, right after Mary's husband died. And when Amy's husband left her, her best friend stopped calling. "The contagious syndrome" propels this behavior, says psychotherapist Xenia Rose, author of *Widow's Journey*. "Whatever disease killed your husband, such people reason, *you* might have it now and could give it to others. No contact means no catching," she says, explaining her term. She also notes the less concrete, but probably more realistic rationale for their abandonment: You've forced your friends to look life straight in the face and showed them that it can blow up at any time for anyone. "People have difficulty dealing with what's happened to you because it rattles their own sense of security and safety. They too will vanish from your life," Rose says.[7] The same explanation holds true in cases of divorce: If your marriage, which looked healthy from the outside, could destruct, so can your friends'. Your divorce makes their marriages seem more vulnerable.

Friends-who-abandon-you represents just one piece of the friendship story for recently divorced and widowed women. We'll explore the other issues that affect their friendships by meeting two women—one a widow and the other divorced—to see how their new status impacts on their connections with other women.

A Widow's Ties

A year ago, **Carol**, fifty-six, who owns a small bookstore, lost her husband Raymond, a newspaper columnist, to cancer. During their fifteen years together—a second marriage for both—Carol considered Ray her best friend and he felt the same way about her. Yet they both had a great deal of autonomy and their own social lives. Following Raymond's death, their friends did not discard Carol. On the contrary: Because of his prominence, many of his colleagues and their casual acquaintances sought her out. "If somebody wants to bring me in just because I lost Raymond, I'm very resistant," she insists, questioning their sincerity. She wants friends to choose her for who *she* is, not because she had a prominent spouse or because they feel sorry for her.

In the wake of his death, Carol has grativated to women. "I don't want to be close to men or have much to do with them, which is surprising, because the theory is that if you had a good marriage you would want to get married again. But I feel much more connected with women. Some of my friends have wonderful husbands, and I like being with the two of them, but my women friends sustain me," she says.

She offers this explanation about why women intrigue her now: "I think I'm nervous and awkward—more awkward than I was when I was divorced, for some reason—with any man alone. I don't feel they're going to rape me. I just don't feel like I want to be open with them. I feel much more like I'm a woman's woman than a man's woman. There's something about women having nurtured their children, or maybe it's the kinds of women I'm drawn to. I feel much freer to be me with women. I feel like we talk a different language. I'm more comfortable in my whole range of emotions around women. I trust their responses."

Carol has not said that she doesn't trust men, only that she feels more comfortable with women. But two men, whom she counted on, left her: her first husband through divorce and the second through death. No doubt, like many widows, she feels angry: "Why me?" "Why am I abandoned again?" "Who said life was fair?" Part of her may also feel relieved to give up her nurturing role. Perhaps she's tired of taking care of sick men. As we discussed in the last chapter, many men at midlife tend to become more dependent on their wives and demand more attention and care. Carol may fear the prospect of nursing another man.

Among Carol's close friends, she sees Claudia, whose husband died four years ago, the most and feels they share the most. Their common loss and status draw them together. "We talk about what it's like to deal with all the strange things that feel like assaults, the insensitivities that only someone who has lost a mate would probably understand. They're not intended that way, but sometimes it's almost a twisted kind of a thing where somebody meant well, but somehow just hit a very, very tender spot," she says.

Carol regards Claudia as a mentor, since she has been a widow longer, and often approaches her for advice. After Carol's husband's death, she wanted her home to feel more comfortable and safer. Claudia told her she turns on the music as soon as she walks in the door. "I tripled that," says Carol. "I bought a little radio with a pocket-size remote so the minute I wake up during the night, I can put the radio on. It's like a friend to me. So we share that kind of information back and forth."

Carol continues, "I've literally asked her for advice about how to structure your time when you're alone. We've also shared books, helped each other decide what to write on our husbands' stones, or discuss what clothes we're going to wear."

In different ways Carol has become a role model for Claudia. Claudia never worked outside the home during her thirty-five-year marriage and relied on her husband to handle their finances and make plans. Carol has run the bookstore for twenty-five years and lived on her own in the years between her divorce and her remarriage. Each woman's background forged her attitude toward widowhood. "I've said to her, 'I'm not waiting for the universe to make this better for me' and she clearly is," Carol told me, obviously upset at Claudia's passivity.

Carol goes on, "She sees me go out and do for myself, yet she's more reluctant. She does things, she travels, but it's more an attitude. 'Why hasn't so-and-so done this?' 'Nobody's calling me.' 'How do I get something going?' " She mimics Claudia's complaints. Claudia feels entitled to special treatment, while Carol realizes that only she can make things happen.

Carol has also found that without her husband's companionship, she must sometimes choose between friends and that this can cause rivalries, reviving memories of adolescent bickering. She invited Claudia to accompany her and her two sisters to Spain. For a trip to the Grand Canyon, however, Carol asked a divorced friend to go along so they could share the driving. (Claudia doesn't drive.) Carol chose her divorced friend for practical reasons, but she knows Claudia will be upset. "This is going to be a problem because I almost feel as if I owe all my offers to Claudia. So when you don't have a partner, a lot of things become very, very tricky among your friends, because some people might feel that they are favorites."

What does Carol, as a new widow, want from her other friends? A willingness to listen when she feels like talking. An acceptance of her grieving process, no matter how fast or slow it happens. An understanding that emotional setbacks crop up unexpectedly and that an innocent remark can spark painful memories. And an offer of specific help. Saying "Call me if you need anything" is too vague. When you're grieving you may not know what you need or have the energy to pick up the phone. Widows appreciate concrete offers, such as "I'll bring you dinner tomorrow" or "I'd like to rake your front yard." Of course, friends cannot eliminate a widow's pain, but offering practical as well as emotional support does ease the transition.

A Divorcee's Connections

New divorcees cope with many of the same issues that widows face: Initially they feel more comfortable and have more in common with other divorced women. They, too, serve as role models and mentors for each other in coping with the effects of their divorces. And again, a positive, can-do attitude makes a tremendous difference in rebuilding a life following divorce.

Barbara, fifty-five, a television producer for a local public affairs show, and her husband Richard divorced last year after thirty-three years of marriage following his affair with a young law student. For two years prior to her divorce she had poured all her emotional energy into saving her marriage and taking care of her aging parents, who both died last summer. Her good friends, a mix of single and married women, talked to her almost every day. They never judged her; they simply listened.

Their support helped Barbara cope with her new life alone. "We talk a lot about the loneliness—two of my married friends have husbands who are ill—and the challenges of doing it on your own. We talk about other people, of course," she says with a laugh. "And we talk about ways to make our lives enjoyable, things we want to do, and certainly our children. We talk about what it's like to navigate on your own. We just try to care for one another. More than anything, you want somebody to listen. With your close friends, you don't want to play games. You don't want to have to cover up things, particularly when you're lonely."

As an afterthought, she adds, again laughing, "I don't have any sex life, so maybe someday when I do, I might not discuss that. I certainly discuss people I've been out with, but I haven't been out with that many men because I haven't been divorced all that long. If I had a relationship that I thought was really important, I probably would discuss it with these close friends."

For Barbara, the sense of isolation since her divorce continues to loom. She misses the peripheral friends, including Richard's partners and her acquaintances from the Junior League who accompanied her status as a prominent attorney's wife. "I don't socialize nearly as much and certainly not with the same group. I miss some of those people. I liked being out and about and involved. My ex-husband had a huge law practice, so there were a lot of people in our lives. He generated much of that, so that's missing. And there's another thing. People go away for the weekends to their mountain house and you tend not to be included because you're not a couple. I don't think they intentionally leave you out. I would imagine most divorced women would notice that."

To compensate for these losses, Barbara has pushed herself to make new friends. "I'm looking to make my world a little bigger. That's probably it more than anything. I'm trying to fill some of those gaps that come with losing a mate and a whole set of legal people. I've seen them for thirty-some-odd years, so I'm looking to fill that void."

Recently Barbara enrolled in a drawing class and signed up for a birding workshop, two longtime interests. In both of these activities, she has met women who have the potential to become confidantes. "It's too early to tell if they'll be good friends," she says, "but I've been looking and reaching out and enjoyed getting to know them."

Lovin' That Man

When a romantic partner enters the life of a single woman, repercussions ripple throughout her friendships. Such issues as how to budget time and energy without shortchanging her friends (or the man) and how to cope with the guilt of abandoning a friend and still feel good about the heterosexual relationship all affect friendships. Difficult as these issues are, almost every woman I interviewed said she would not sacrifice a female friendship for a man today, as she might have done at a younger age. "My women friends are very important to me. They're tried-and-true. Men come and go," says **Cindy,** speaking for many midlife women. "As I've gotten older, I've learned that women are the ones who will be there and I don't want to jeopardize a relationship with a woman for a man."

That said, Cindy also acknowledges that a major relationship with a man will take priority over a friendship with a woman. She tries to keep her connections with friends, however, when she's involved with a man. That can be challenging if he demands a lot of her time. For that reason, she prefers men who have an independent life so that she can maintain her life and her own friends while engaged in a romantic relationship. When she tries to include her single friends in an activity with her partner, they both end up feeling cheated, because each wants her undivided attention.

Juggling a boyfriend and women friends becomes particularly difficult if she hasn't been involved in a romantic relationship for a while, because her close friends have truly become her "significant others." Cindy says, "I'll feel guilty that I'm not doing as much with the woman friend I'm closest with. She'll keep calling and say, 'Do you want to do such and such?' I'll say, 'It's the weekend, I've gotta be with my boyfriend.' "

Cindy tries to be honest about her dilemma but still feels like she's jilting her friends. "It's not that they don't understand on an intellectual level," she says, "but I can tell that they feel hurt because they're used to having me."

Cindy understands exactly how they feel, because she's been on the other side as well. "I feel the same way if a friend who I spend a lot of time with all of a sudden has a boyfriend. You say, 'Oh, that's great for you,' but there's a part of you that thinks, 'I better find myself another friend to do things with.' Your issues of being alone kick in, and if this friend was always there for you, you think, 'Gee, I wonder if now she'll be there for me if I really need her.' "

Cindy spoke honestly about her distress when Mona, a close friend, began a relationship that looked like it might become serious. "There's a piece of me that almost says, 'Gee, I hope I can find some flaw in him so that I don't feel . . . so imperfect.' I don't know why it worries me that she's going to be with this perfect man. I guess because I know my man isn't going to be as perfect," she says, laughing. "I wish I could say that I'm thrilled that she found a man, but I'm not."

It's normal to have such mixed feelings when a close friend becomes involved in a relationship. Of course, Cindy wants Mona to be happy. But another part of her hopes the relationship will fizzle out so Mona won't abandon her. Perhaps Mona will recognize her boyfriend's shortcoming, Cindy thinks; then the relationship won't work out, and she'll have Mona to herself again. Cindy feels guilty even entertaining such selfish thoughts. Nonetheless, these feelings are very real and not at all uncommon.

Part of Cindy's discomfort also stems from not knowing whether Mona's new partner will accept her or if he'll jeopardize their friendship. When she was younger, Cindy had experiences, as did many of us, of friends discarding her as soon as they became romantically involved. "I don't know if this man will allow her to be in my life. I don't know him. Maybe he'll affect her so she won't want to be friends with me," Cindy worries. "Ideally I like it when they both want me in their lives. As I get to know him, if I feel that he's a good person, and he's going to include me, then I feel a lot better about their relationship."

Only one woman, who is currently living with a man, spoke of not feeling "safe" with certain single friends around her partner. She recognizes that her fears stem from getting burned by a couple of friends who had brief flings with her ex-husband while they were married. "I have to know that any single friends have their own life or have their own outside interests as far as men goes," she explains. "I'm less generous if I'm not sure where they're coming from. I'm not necessarily open with them about the reasons why I don't want them a part of my life, but I'm clear about not wanting to open the friendship to them," she says. Wistfully, she adds, "I wish I had done that before."

Bonding with Married Friends

All through Sally's separation and divorce proceedings, her neighbor and good friend Pam sat beside her and listened as she poured out her heart about her failing marriage and her cheating husband. Pam would go home to her husband exhausted and drained but heartened that she could help Sally in her time of need. Once the messy divorce was final, Pam looked forward to playing tennis and going antiquing with Sally again. But much to Pam's surprise, as soon as the divorce came through, Sally stopped calling, waved from across their double driveway, and went on her way, off with a new group of friends, all single.

Such a scenario is not uncommon. We talked earlier of how married couples may drop a newly divorced or widowed woman; the reverse also happens. Married friends can remind a recent widow or divorcee of her life with her husband, which she may want to forget. She's ready to move on and start over. Being with a married woman can also accentuate her singleness. If she goes out with her friend and her husband, she either feels like a third wheel or focuses on the empty chair at the table and feels her loss more acutely. While it can be comforting to know someone who *lived* her history and knows exactly what she means when she speaks of her ex, initially that fact matters less than being with women in similar circumstances.

Friendships between single and married women can present a challenge—or not, depending on your perspective. Whether such friendships work depends on the individuals involved. Some single women think being friends with a married woman is like the color of one's eyes, a fact of life that has no impact on friendship. Nan, a fifty-one-year-old divorced management consultant says, "Single people have just as many troubles as people who are married," she says, laughing. "We all screw up the same things, basically. There's no difference in tears being spilled over somebody's boyfriend or someone's husband." She chuckles again.

Does she share different things with single friends than with married ones? "I don't make those distinctions. I don't say to my friends who have partners, 'Oh, you wouldn't understand because you're married.' We've known each other when we had partners or were married or single, so we just *know* each other. I am not attracted to people because of their partner status, so to speak."

Another divorced woman feels differently, however. "I do think that single women talk among themselves differently than a single woman talks with a married friend," Sandra told me. "I know with my single friends, we get more explicit about sex and dating than we do with our married friends. And the single women I know who've had an affair with a married man rarely shared that information with married friends. Why, I'm not sure, but probably because they don't want them to worry that it could happen to them. Also, there's a bit of guilt, I guess."

Nonetheless, befriending a married woman has its benefits. If she has children and you don't, you can feel a sense of family, participate in their celebrations, and develop special connections with her children. If you are divorced or widowed, with children of your own, joining another family for holiday dinners can extend yours and help you feel less isolated.

Coping with Differences

Friendships between single and married women do have their challenges, however. Having a male partner creates fundamental lifestyle differences. Married women must share their attention, their energy, and their time. They are usually less available to go to dinner or the movies. An unmarried woman without children doesn't have such divided loyalties or logistical hassles. It's less complicated to associate with other singles, because they implicitly understand each other's life and lifestyle.

Sometimes, however, the differences do not run as deep as they appear. Cindy feels she could not reveal to Geena, a married friend with a grown daughter, how inadequate Cindy feels because she never had children. While Geena might not share that precise situation, certainly she could empathize with the feeling of inadequacy and relate it to times in her life when she felt she short-changed her daughter or disappointed her husband. Beneath their lifestyle differences, these two women share a deeply held feeling, which could draw them closer if they were able to discuss it openly.

Cindy also spoke earlier of how at times she feels ashamed of being single. If she were able to tell Geena how she envies her stable home, Geena might confide that she covets Cindy's carefree, independent life and fantasizes about running away. Talking about their longings can prevent their feelings from becoming entangled in envy, or worse, in self-disgust. Their discussion won't eliminate either one's distress, but it moves the focus away from envy and self-hatred to their own desires. Instead of berating themselves for their longings, they can help each other accept them and, perhaps, find some way to fulfill some of them.[8]

For a friendship to succeed between a single and married woman, the married woman needs a degree of autonomy. She has to feel free to make plans on her own, see her friends independently, and not feel guilty about leaving her husband. Carol, the new widow, will only befriend married women who have such freedom. "I have a harder time feeling close to someone who never does things without her husband," she says.

At the same time single women told me they need to feel accepted by their married friends' husbands and expect them to be cordial on the phone and welcoming when they visit. One woman feels good when she can claim both husband and wife as friends, although that matters less to all single women. Ultimately, for the friendship to work, both women need to be flexible and sensitive to lifestyle differences and willing to make compromises.

Building a Network

Being single does not necessarily mean being lonely. Yet fear of loneliness drives women to avoid the single life at all costs, forcing some to remain in flat, loveless marriages. But according to researchers Anderson and Stewart, loneliness was such a "minor concern" among the single women in their study that few even raised the topic. Women told them that the anticipation of loneliness was far more "powerful and terrifying" than the reality.[9]

Of course, single women feel lonely from time to time. So do married women. Unmarried women cope with these periods, say Anderson and Stewart, by calling friends, diving into a project, or just "riding" through the emotions. Some women were able to take command of their loneliness by reframing their perspective. Rather than seeing time alone as a negative, they began to view it as a resource, a natural part of life and a benefit of being on their own. In essence, they learned to appreciate solitude.

One of the best ways to combat lengthy periods of solitude—unless we choose this—is to build a strong network. Christine, whose story opened this chapter, says her inner circle feels complete with three close friends. Someone else would find such a small circle insufficient and confining. Other women I interviewed told me they need a nucleus of five or six close friends as well as several casual acquaintances with similar interests to see occasionally, and colleagues from work, male and female.

Each woman must create a network that fits her needs and preferences in terms of size, diversity of marital status and background, and proximity. If her network feels full and whole, however narrow it appears, then it is. Generally, though, the strength of a single woman's network lies in its breadth and diversity. All her emotional eggs are not in one basket. If one breaks, the entire network will not collapse.

At our age, chances are a tie will splinter because of illness or death rather than because of conflict. Seeing a friend develop breast cancer or another illness at midlife forces us to confront our own vulnerabilities. If something could happen to *her,* it could also happen to *me.* That prospect raises another set of anxieties for single women: Who will offer practical help if I am incapacitated? Who will lend moral support, to listen to my worries and anxieties? Fear of facing their elder years alone pushes single women to build a strong network *now* for protection later in their old age.

Chapter Six

When Illness Strikes

"Your truest friends are those who visit you in prison or in hospital."

Moroccan proverb

In Elizabeth Berg's book *Talk Before Sleep,* Ann Stanley puts her own life on hold to be with her best friend, Ruth, who is dying of cancer. When they met a few years earlier, Ann told herself that she could "forgive" Ruth her good looks, because Ruth "was capable of a scary kind of honesty I was ready for, although until that moment, I hadn't realized how much I'd been needing to meet someone I might be able to say everything to."[1]

Throughout the book the two friends do discuss everything: their work, their marriages, their disappointments, their hopes and dreams—just as we do with our close friends. But their dialogues run deeper and contain a candor and a poignancy because we know—as do they—that Ruth will die. One minute they are discussing funeral arrangements and the next gossiping. Whether they are gorging themselves on hot fudge sundaes heaped with whipped cream or sharing memories and confidences, Ann's unconditional love for Ruth shines through. As Ruth's condition worsens, Ann doesn't coddle her or overprotect her. She is simply there: a constant, accepting, often irreverent, presence in Ruth's life. A loyal, devoted friend.

Inevitably, as we age, either we or one of our friends will face serious illness. That thought alone rocks our very foundation. Whether breast cancer, heart trouble, or another disease, illness alters our life and all our relationships, and can certainly destabilize a friendship. Women who have been both patient and friend will speak as we examine the ramifications of illness on friendship. Will the friendship survive the illness, and if so, in what form? Who will remain a friend and who will withdraw? What kind of support truly helps? Some of us, like Ann, will also have to say good-bye to a dying friend—never an easy task. Mourning becomes even more difficult in a culture that belittles our loss, because she's "just a friend."

A Special Bonding

In 1989, David Spiegel, M.D., a professor of psychiatry and behavioral sciences at the Stanford University School of Medicine, published the results of his study on the effects of group therapy on the quality of life of patients with metastatic breast cancer. During the yearlong project, all patients received routine medical care. Those in the treatment group also participated in group psychotherapy, while those in the control group did not. Not only did the treatment group experience an improved quality of life but they lived longer. The more support they received, the longer they lived—as much as eighteen months longer than the control group.[2]

Since Dr. Spiegel's groundbreaking research, two other studies have reached similar conclusions. Jean Richardson, a psychologist at the University of Southern California, offered counseling and home visits to patients with lymphomas and leukemias. They, too, outlived the control group. Fawzy I. Fawzy, a psychiatrist at the University of California at Los Angeles, randomly assigned malignant-skin-cancer patients to support groups; those who participated in groups were less moody and coped better. In a follow-up study done six years later, Dr. Fawzy found that those assigned to support groups had experienced a longer time between recurrences and that fewer had died.[3]

We cannot assume that if support groups produced such positive results, then support from friends would have similar benefits. But these dramatic studies do reveal the importance of sharing emotions, particularly with someone who has the same disease. Not everyone with breast cancer has access to a support group or the time or inclination to participate; but talking about our experiences and feelings with a good friend does help the sick person feel less isolated and more comforted.

When **Betsy,** fifty-seven, an interior decorator, learned she had breast cancer in the lobules, not in the ducts as most women do, she thought it sounded very much like what her friend Gail, also fifty-seven, had had two years before. "When Gail was diagnosed, I heard it, but I didn't feel it. I didn't truly understand it," Betsy remembers. "I felt sad. I wished I could help her, but I didn't know what to do. I remember admiring her bravery and her wonderful attitude. It was her attitude that pulled me immediately to her. I wanted to share that and I needed to hear those positive things."

After going through a harrowing week of meetings with breast surgeons to get second and third opinions, she called Gail, who had been a close friend since fourth grade. They had remained tight through high school and college and Gail's divorce, even though she had moved to Tucson five years ago. Betsy still lives in Baltimore.

When they talked, Betsy learned that indeed, the two women had the exact same diagnosis. Gail had undergone a double mastectomy and reconstructive surgery, as Betsy planned to do. "We had this instant level of communication, and I had to run everything by her: 'How did you feel about this?' 'How did you go through that?'" Betsy recalls. "She was coming to Baltimore within a few weeks and couldn't wait to show me her reconstruction so I'd know what to expect. It was a special bonding. She helped me through my experience step by step by step.

"Then after I had surgery and was talking about recovery, I had more questions, because reconstruction has its own set of physical and emotional challenges," Betsy continues. "We talked about diet, exercise, meditation, nutritional supplements. We encouraged each other to do things to enhance our quality of life. Eventually, we got to the point where we started worrying about the rest of our lives."

Betsy became involved in the breast cancer movement and started playing an activist role. "Gail learned that part from me. And I listened to her very carefully about the nurturing part, about how she began to meditate. We always checked in with each other," Betsy recalls. "At one point she decided that her implants were more bothersome and disfiguring than helpful and said, 'I don't need these anymore. It's not important to me.' So she had them removed. Then she appeared in Baltimore and said, 'Look at me. I'm absolutely flat, and I'm perfectly happy.' I admire that."

Twelve years have passed since Gail's diagnosis; ten for Betsy. Both remain healthy. They still visit each other twice a year. "This is a very, very strong bond, and it's truly sisterhood. It is an emotional, physical, and spiritual bond that connects us," Betsy believes.

Betsy shares a special connection with Gail, yet because they live so far apart, Betsy recognized that she needed support on a daily basis as well. Since her diagnosis she has turned to other women in Baltimore who have breast cancer. "You can be very open without worrying about frightening your friends [who aren't sick]," she says, recollecting how she felt when another friend was diagnosed a year before she learned of her own cancer. "I remember being with her right after her diagnosis and it was this attraction/repulsion thing: I want to help you but I really don't want to get too close, because I'm frightened about it myself."

Running Scared

The aura of fear surrounding breast cancer and other serious diseases comes from the same place as the fear that causes people to desert their friends who get divorced or widowed. If cancer, divorce, or death can strike someone we're close to, it can hit us, too. When we read about these events in the newspaper or see them on television, they seem distant and disconnected from our lives. They don't touch us personally in the same way as a friend's illness does.

The unspoken fear is that a friend's disease will contaminate our world. Up until now, we felt safe and secure. Disease reminds us that we are human, fallible, that we can be felled by disease at any time. It's not that we didn't know that on some level or that we thought we were immortal, but we were not consciously confronting these ideas every day.

Dealing with the ramifications of illness is depressing. How painful to watch someone we care about suffer. While we hope for the best, the prospect of losing a friend with whom we share a twenty- or thirty-year history, who has been a witness to our lives and we to hers, is shattering. We fear not only losing her but forfeiting the future with her. We want to grow old together.

If our lives are going well, we don't want to think about all the misfortunes that can befall us. Why rock the boat? I am considering a writing project on a topic related to breast cancer. While it sounds fascinating, I also question whether I want to work on a topic that no doubt will frighten and depress me. I'm interested in how women live with cancer day by day, but a part of me doesn't want to know about those day-to-day challenges. Out of sight, out of mind. Working with women with breast cancer will remind me that I am just as vulnerable as the next woman.

These fears are all too common and perfectly normal. Ideally, we can recognize them, then push them aside to rush to the aid of a friend who is ill. But not everyone can do that: Their fears loom too large. Betsy had a very painful experience with another friend whom she would have defined as her very best buddy before she—Betsy—took sick. Their connection stretched back to college. "Clair and I had a very close, laughing, sharing-on-a-cerebral-and-soulful-level kind of relationship. We were really in touch. We shared a quirky point of view. We traveled together as couples. It was a very important relationship to me," Betsy remembers. Yet she adds that Clair had always been a very private person and had begun distancing herself from Betsy shortly before her diagnosis. Although Betsy could not pinpoint a specific turning point, she sensed that something had begun to shift in their relationship.

When Betsy was selecting a breast surgeon, she asked Clair to accompany her to a consultation. Betsy recalls that day: "I remember her sitting there with me and knitting while I waited. I'm chatting away, trying to make the time feel safer and a little bit more normal. I went in to see the doctor alone. My other friend had gone in with me, as had my husband. Clair stayed in the waiting room. That particular physician interview was very unsatisfactory, and I left so angry. Clair really didn't respond much or emote when I voiced my frustration. She was not 'into' it. She just was avoiding the issue."

To Betsy, Clair seemed indifferent and withholding. But the truth is, we don't really know what Clair was experiencing. Perhaps *she* would have been uncomfortable with a friend sitting in on her consultation; maybe Clair assumed Betsy did not want her there. If Betsy needed Clair to accompany her, Betsy should have said so. Each woman was operating from her individual perspective.

After Betsy's surgery, Clair did not contact her, so Betsy called her. "Clair said, 'Oh, I just haven't had a chance to call.' I responded, 'I have to say this: I'm very hurt. I've been home a week and you're very close to me. I need to see you. Just pick up a couple of sandwiches and come for lunch.' " Clair told her that she had been sick while visiting her son in New York and that her own illness had sapped all her energy. Betsy said she honored that but felt that Clair's explanation did not justify her aloofness.

"She just wasn't there with me emotionally. I thought something happened. Either this kicks into her own concerns and fears or she just doesn't want to be sucked into my problems," Betsy says. After this, they saw each other occasionally, but the warmth had completely disappeared. Eventually, Betsy says, "We just drifted apart. She went through an illness that I didn't even know about and felt very bad about learning after the fact. When I went to see her, she was so cool that I realized that our relationship had ended."

Betsy heard through the grapevine that Clair had sold her house and moved to a condominium in another neighborhood. On days when Betsy feels generous she tells herself that maybe Clair wanted to start a new phase of her life. But, for a long time, Betsy says, "I felt sad and hurt. This had been a very central, important relationship to me."

Few women forget the sting of rejection, especially if it strikes when they already feel vulnerable. But we need to be sensitive to the fact that everyone can't give as we'd like. Maybe Clair just learned that her husband was having an affair and didn't want to burden Betsy while she was sick. Or perhaps Clair had just placed her eighty-year-old mother in a nursing home and felt so depleted, she had nothing left to give Betsy. Whatever the reason for Clair's aloofness, it would have been helpful if she and Betsy could talk about it—not an unreasonable expectation in light of their long history.

But what kind of dialogue can you engage in with a friend who is ill? Is she emotionally available for any kind of give-and-take? When you're sick, it's often difficult to be there for a friend. And you might even wonder why you need to be available for anyone else. But, even in sickness, we need to be able to listen, to take some of the focus off ourselves. Certainly, Betsy would have been more understanding and less disappointed if she could have heard Clair explain what motivated her detachment. Unfortunately, though, we may never learn why a friend does not come through.

Pitching In

Most of the time we stand by our sick friends. We push our fears or personal concerns aside and pitch in. Even though we may not understand or empathize in the same way as someone who suffers with the same illness, by midlife most of us have dealt with sickness of our own or in a family member. We know the upheaval it can bring to our sense of self and to our relationships. Usually such experiences enable us to reach out to a friend in need. "A couple of my friends had breast cancer and I was able to support them," a forty-nine-year-old suburban woman told me. "Five or ten years ago I would have withdrawn, partly because I wouldn't know what to do and partly because I had no model for handling that kind of situation."

Friends help in very practical ways. When a stroke felled **Maureen,** the fifty-year-old owner of a boutique in Santa Fe, she wasn't able to walk or drive and could hardly talk. At the time she was working full-time and enrolled in an MBA program at night. She hired someone to manage the shop, but she was determined not to give up her course work. She and her daughter, an undergraduate student, had dreamed of graduating together. A month after her diagnosis, she had recovered enough to sit in class and tape a lecture; her handwriting still looked like gibberish. Every week Maureen's friends took turns driving her to the university, an hour away. Each night they delivered a homemade dinner. They accompanied her to medical appointments and consoled her when her frustrations drove her to tears. When Maureen and her daughter graduated six months later, her friends threw a party for them.

You would think that such an independent, ambitious woman would have difficulty accepting help. "At first I didn't have any energy to really experience those kind of emotions," Maureen says. "My illness affected everything. It took too much energy to be happy, sad, grateful, or embarrassed. It just was beyond me. Then, as I began to get a little bit better, I was dealing with so much—redefining who I was and trying to come to a positive understanding about how this had affected my life—that I realized that if I received my friends graciously, the joy that they had in giving would not be diminished. So I chose not to be embarrassed or upset," she recalls. "Their support humbled me. It made me feel very grateful."

While some women may fear being a burden or creating resentment among their friends, Maureen did not. She prevented this from happening by giving back emotionally to her friends, even while she was sick. She was openly grateful and offered genuine thanks. She also listened to her friends and stayed involved in their lives.

Not only did Maureen's friends provide practical help, but they listened as day after day she shared her frustrations and anxieties about her condition. "It was painful [to hear]," says Judy, one of the women in Maureen's inner circle, "because we knew how important being active was to her. She also went through a lot psychologically, because she felt she had lost the things that made her attractive. She is a very attractive person, not vain at all, and at first she had some paralysis around the mouth and couldn't feel her hands. She had a hard time putting lipstick on without getting it down in the corners of her mouth."

Her friends had planned a women-only getaway weekend to San Diego prior to her illness and decided to go ahead with the trip even though Maureen was not doing well. "She slowed down the group. But we took turns spending time with her and walking more slowly and not doing things, so she wouldn't feel like she wasn't up to speed. But it definitely made a difference," Judy recalls. After a pause she adds softly, "We would not have gone without her." Maureen's friends would not continue being so generous if they weren't also receiving something from her. A friendship cannot sustain itself unless everyone feels like a winner.

Enhancing Your Support

Maureen does not need advice on how to accept her friends' assistance graciously. There are ways, however, for someone who is ill to enhance the support of her friends and family, says Dr.

David Spiegel, who has worked extensively with women in breast cancer support groups.

Dr. Spiegel recommends that women who are ill choose their supportive network carefully. "Save your energy," he says, "and use the illness as an excuse to disengage from unwanted social obligations. Simplify the relationships that are necessary but un-rewarding, and eliminate the ones that are unnecessary *and* un-rewarding." Then keep those you've chosen for your network informed. He believes that you strengthen mutual caring and cop-ing by sharing information, including the serious consequences of your illness.

You can help your friends further by telling them just what they can do for you. Many people feel uncomfortable asking for help, but if you can suggest that you need a ride to a medical appointment or would appreciate a dinner once a month, your friends will probably be happy to comply. Putting these sugges-tions into practice may feel like another burden on top of being ill, but doing so will help you feel more in control and you'll get the kind of help you most need. You'll also gain a sense that you are participating in—not just taking from—the relationship.

Offering Aid

Maureen's friends know how to care for a sick friend. They followed their hearts, with their loyalty and affection for Maureen guiding them. But everyone who wants to offer help does not know how to go about it. Many times friends and acquaintances will rally after the diagnosis and send cards, flowers, or gifts. But as the illness wears on, people desperately want to get back to their lives, and do. That happened to a single, childless woman who lost a pregnancy in her early forties. She remembers, "My friends stuck by me at the loss and right after, but when I didn't bounce back, I lost my main circle of friends," she recalls. "My grief was just too dark for them. They couldn't understand and felt I was not getting better quickly enough. At that point it was so hard having people around me who misjudged me that it was easier to let them go."

Ideally, your friends will stay the course. Barbara DeLuca, executive program director of the Linda Creed Breast Cancer Foundation in Philadelphia, advises women who have a sick friend: "The most important kind of support is just being available, being able to sit beside someone and listen—not saying 'What can I do to help?' but thinking of ways to be helpful. It's hard for women in general, and for women with breast cancer in particular, to ask for help. We are not used to requesting attention or assistance, but it certainly feels good when flowers or gifts or food or loving messages come in."

She suggests, "Do the proactive thing that shows that you're sensitive to [your friend's] needs and want to help. Just be at the door with dinner. Say, 'Let me drive you to the doctor's.' Offer your ear and make it clear you're really open to listening. Or send a card that says 'I love you and I'm thinking about you' without asking for anything or giving anything, but letting friends know that they're in your thoughts. Just honor the friendship and think of what needs can be met. You're not trying to solve the big problem."

Barbara DeLuca adds a word of caution. "Giving advice never feels good. If someone expresses an interest in complementary or alternative medicine, for example, and says, 'Have you heard of such and such or do you know about this new concept?' then you can do some research that would help them. Ask around, come up with information, and fulfill the request," she says. "But offering advice often sounds like you're saying 'You *should* be doing this' or 'You *shouldn't* be doing that.' That never feels good. Follow the lead of the woman who's going through it. Listen carefully. And just be present."

If you're not particularly close to the person who is sick but would like to show your concern by offering a hand, DeLuca recommends, "Follow your instincts. Do what you feel you want to do, not what's right or wrong." Reaching out to someone you don't know well may transform an acquaintance into a real friend. On the other hand, a friend who had cancer years ago told me, "My illness was the nail in the coffin for marginal friends who didn't show. If they weren't there when I was sick, I knew they'd never be there." Sociologist Jan Yager, Ph.D., agrees. She says, "Coming through for others . . . may not guarantee you are, or will become, better friends, but *failing* to come through may stop that relationship in its tracks."[4]

A System of Caring

Marian and **Jean,** both fifty-five, grew up together in upstate New York. Their mothers were best friends and the two girls were inseparable until they turned twelve and Jean's family moved to Manhattan. Over the years Jean and Marian ran into each other at parties and reunions, but with busy careers and families, they never spent enough time together to recapture the special connection they enjoyed as girls.

About five years ago Jean's eighty-two-year-old mother asked her to organize and catalog the family photos, which were bulging from cartons in Jean's basement. Jean knew Marian had completed a similar project for her family and called her. They started spending time together, sifting through old photos. Before long they were catching up on decades of each other's life. Jean longed for the sister she never had; Marian talked to her sister only twice a year. "Our ability to understand each other was absolutely amazing. It was just uncanny," Jean says. "When people would ask me what she wants or needs, I just knew." In less than a year each considered the other her best friend.

Six months later Marian was diagnosed with lung cancer, which rapidly spread through her entire body. "When she started with the doctors, I would go and listen to what they had to say and what she had to say, and try to facilitate her asking questions," recalls Jean. "Often she would call me about things that were bothering her. One time after her chemo, she really sounded weird. I thought she needed medical attention immediately, so I told her to call her internist. Having control was very important to her. The hardest thing for me was that she did a lot of things her way, not my way. I learned a lot from that."

As Marian got progressively sicker, Jean spoke to Marian's daughters without her knowledge. Jean told them in so many words, "Your mom is really sick and I think she's going to die and soon." One of the daughters, who was not aware of how ill her mother was, wrote a letter that Jean took to Marian in the hospital. The other became hysterical at the news. Jean encouraged Marian to talk to her, suggesting, "Why don't you see if she has anything to say or has any questions. You just came back from chemo and she wants to know what's going on." After their discussion her daughter became more nurturing toward her mother.

When Marian was hospitalized, Jean devised a system for Marian's friends to help. She called Millie, one of Marian's closest friends, and the two of them developed a master list of Marian's friends. They divided every day of the week into three shifts and assigned a friend to each shift so Marian would never be alone. Everyone checked in with Jean or Millie before they went to the hospital. "She didn't want to be alone, and yet she didn't necessarily want people to talk to her. Often she couldn't talk. So we picked friends who could just go and sit," Jean says.

"I would call her the night before I went in and see if she needed anything—yogurt, potatoes, coffee—then I would always call before I left home. She didn't want to hear about anybody sick or dying or having problems. She was really too sick. So we covered her needs that way."

Marian's husband accepted her huge network of friends as a necessary presence in their life. He knew they mattered enormously to her. Jean says, "My husband would never tolerate friends coming in, caring, and arranging things. So my friends would never do that but Marian's [husband] did."

The week before Marian died, Jean had to go out of town on business. Before she left, she called Millie and said, "If she dies, call everybody on the list . . . I'm really okay." At that point the women supporting Marian were, in fact, all supporting each other. "I knew Marian would not die until I came home," Jean said. Marian died two days after Jean returned to town.

Saying Good-bye

Jean showed her love for Marian by the way she arranged a schedule for her friends to visit so Marian would not be alone during her final months. Marian knew she cared, but they did not actually say good-bye. Marian wouldn't allow it. Everyone around her had to be upbeat and she didn't want to hear any depressing news, especially about anyone else's health. Jean recalls, "Marian didn't make it easy for her friends. She didn't give people a chance to say good-bye. Toward the end she would let me tuck her in, fluff her pillow, sit her up, which she would never allow before. Before I left, that [last] day I held her hand while she was getting the treatment. We talked a little bit. 'We're going to miss you,' I did say. I think we both knew that this was it."

There is probably nothing more difficult than saying good-bye to someone who is dying. You worry that you'll say the wrong thing, upset the other person, or worse yet, cry. Yet not saying anything or not showing emotion may appear as indifference, say Maggie Callanan and Patricia Kelley, two hospice nurses who have each worked over twenty years with the dying.[5] They say it's fine to cry together if that's how you genuinely feel.

Callanan and Kelley stress taking the cue from the person who is dying, as Jean did. Marian sent strong signals that she did not want to discuss her impending death. Perhaps she was not ready to talk, didn't have the energy, or preferred to talk to a family member. Or she may have wanted to spare Jean. Although Jean never told Marian in words how much she mattered to her, Jean's constant presence demonstrated her devotion to Marian and her loyalty to their friendship.

Let the dying person know you are interested and willing to talk and then let the conversation develop, Callanan and Kelley advise. They suggest beginning with a simple comment, such as "I'm sorry to hear that you're so ill" or "I really feel sad when I think about what's happening to you." Then wait for a response. Once your friend begins talking, listen.

You might also talk about the life you've shared, recalling special times or amusing anecdotes. When you do this, you show your friend that she and the relationship mattered to you. Without actually saying that you'll miss her, you are telling her that she'll be remembered. No one wants to be forgotten.

"There is no one right thing to say, although it's never wrong to speak of your love and concern," say the hospice nurses. "Don't worry about saying or doing the 'wrong' thing . . . What's often

harder to forgive—whether for the dying person or in one's self—
is the failure to do so or say anything."[6]

Mourning a Friend

Alice, fifty-one, a divorced yoga instructor, lost two close
friends within the span of a month. One of the women who died
came regularly to her yoga studio, so people in class talked about
her constantly, which gave Alice an opportunity to process the
death and review their friendship. The other death, that of a longtime neighbor, Alice shared with another neighbor. They fast-
walked together twice a week, so had plenty of opportunity to
discuss their common loss. Alice also belonged to a women's support group. Two women in the group had lost friends as well, so
they understood Alice's need to talk about her feelings at their
weekly meetings.

Alice was fortunate to get the support she needed following the
deaths of two friends. Women don't always receive permission to
mourn a friend. Without a label such as "widow" or "orphan,"
grieving friends are often left to mourn on their own. Sociologists
Fred Sklar and Shirley F. Hartley argue that the number of
survivor-friends is growing as the population ages, yet they remain
invisible, silently mourning the deaths of their close friends.[7]
While a friend's grief can be as intense as a family member's, it
is not generally recognized, acknowledged, or socially supported.[8]
Many social service agencies offer support groups for widows,
including specialized groups for widows under fifty and those over
fifty, but I've never heard of a support group for friends of the
deceased.

In the two small-scale studies Sklar and Hartley conducted,
they found that mourning friends may be at greater risk for social,

emotional, and health problems than grieving family members, because friends do not receive the support they need to do the emotional work of bereavement. "Survivor-friends might be allowed to be unhappy for a short period following a death, but that is all," the sociologists say. "Other friends and family of the survivor-friend typically do not want to hear about their grief, especially if there is a sense of competition about loyalty."[9]

Thus, a husband becomes impatient when his wife doesn't snap out of her sadness within a week or two of a friend's death. He wonders, What's taking her so long? After all, she was "just a friend." As we've seen, however, the emotional involvement in a close or best friendship can be as deep and intense as the investment in a marriage. For a single woman, the friendship may be the most significant relationship in her life. Grieving friends experience the same kind of loneliness and need for support as do those who lose any meaningful intimate relationship.[10]

The results of these studies remind us that we need to support friends grieving for other friends and allow them to mourn in their own way and at their own pace. There is no right or wrong way to grieve, or a set timetable. One woman may need weeks; another, months or even years. It helps to remember the five stages of grieving, described by physician Elizabeth Kubler-Ross in her book *On Death and Dying*. Everyone goes through periods of denial, anger, bargaining, depression, and eventually acceptance—although not necessarily in that order. We can comfort a grieving friend by simply being there and listening.

The Legacy of Loss

When a friend dies in her twenties or thirties, we are saddened, shocked, and indignant at the unfairness of a young life cut short.

When we lose a friend at midlife, we may feel exactly the same way. But now our response also occurs on a much more personal level. A death at midlife shakes our very being and raises existential questions for our own lives. We wonder: How much time do *I* have left? And how do *I* want to live the years ahead?

A study of thirty-eight women between the ages of sixty-seven and ninety-two by Karen Roberto, professor and coordinator of the gerontology program at the University of Northern Colorado at Greeley, and Pat Stanis of the same university, found that when the women's close friends died, the majority sensed an increased awareness of their own aging and of their own mortality and developed a deeper gratitude for their own lives. One half of the women also reported a greater appreciation for their other friends[11] and a desire to develop closer relationships with them.[12]

While the women in this research project are older than those in my study, the women I interviewed expressed similar sentiments following the death of a close friend. Jean, who arranged the visitation system for her best friend Marian's final days, expressed a new appreciation for living in the moment. "That experience brought life to people. We're not here forever," she says. "Do today whatever you can. Don't put it off to tomorrow . . . Enjoy it."

Another woman, who recently lost two friends, said, "Life is about what you receive through the gift of love. I strive in my friendships to share that gift, because that's what it's really about. To the extent that you can express that love in any material way, then that's just a perk. Other than that, I think the gift of love is the best."

A third women said, "It [the death] really woke me up to the importance of friends in my life. I made a resolution at that point that I would never again take them for granted. I make time to call and visit with them. I make sure that I touch base with them at least once a week, if not more often. And I just make a special point of telling people or showing them how much their friendship means to me."

The loss of a friend reminds us how precious true friends are and gives us pause to reconsider the status of each of our friendships. Dr. David Spiegel's wise words of advice to women with breast cancer are worth repeating: "Simplify the relationships that are necessary but unrewarding, and eliminate the ones that are unnecessary *and* unrewarding." Not an easy thing to do. But if we're able to accomplish that, we are then free to concentrate on the relationships that matter most and deepen those core connections.

Chapter Seven

Deepening or Dissolving Ties

"My task is to simplify and then go deeper, making a commitment . . . To care and polish what remains till it glows and comes alive from loving care."

Sue Bender, *Plain and Simple*

I am walking on the beach with Bonnie, a close friend for almost fifteen years. It's mid-July and we've escaped to the Jersey shore for a few days by ourselves. We fast-walk together at home during the week, so it's not as if we don't talk often, yet being away from our normal routine with the whole day stretching before us has slowed our dialogue. She automatically slides to my left and we hit our stride. We start by chatting about the beach houses we pass, move on to discuss our kids, and as we continue, water splashing around our ankles and the sun beating on our backs, we discuss our regrets as mothers: all the "woulda, coulda, shoul-das" of raising our children. Things we may have thought but never told anyone before.

I know whatever grievous error I think I committed Bonnie will accept and she knows that I will listen to her and validate her feelings as well. No judgments and no criticism. We also know that our conversation will be safe with each other. I am certain she won't repeat what I said to *anyone* and she knows the same about me.

I expect such trust from the women in my inner circle, my tried-and-true friends. I feel connected to every one of them, love each in her own way, and confide in all of them. We all share a common heritage, a similar socioeconomic background, and are close in age, but in many areas we think, behave, and feel differently. I try to accept every one for who she is, knowing that I'm far from perfect. I'm also aware that I must do my part to preserve these friendships or they'll wither away.

Forty-eight of the fifty women I interviewed also possess a circle of close friends. Once accepted into the inner sanctum, however, we don't automatically receive a lifetime guarantee for membership. In fact, at midlife, I believe, each of us, either consciously or unconsciously, reevaluates her friendships. The process often begins innocently enough. You're preparing a guest list for your fiftieth birthday party. Or you think back about who supported you after your father died, or you can only invite ten people to your son's wedding. At times like these, we assess who our true friends are.

Often this assessment comes after careful consideration, but at other times we just snap: "That's it. I've had enough." If we choose to stay, we then must decide how broadly we wish to be involved and how deeply we want to relate. Ideally, each of us remains committed to the relationship, but sometimes the priorities or lifestyle of one of us changes as we age. Many of us let go of peripheral friends at this stage and concentrate on building stronger bonds with those who matter most to us. One woman told me that when she was planning a party, she decided not to include any "marginal" friends. She only invited those with whom she had meaningful, positive connections. At times we must evaluate whether to dissolve a friendship entirely or hold on to fragments of the original bond. Whichever we choose, we need to find ways to disengage gracefully and compassionately.

Strengthening Trust

The trust Bonnie and I share took years to build, but we nudge the process along each time we self-disclose. The very act of sharing our fears and anxieties and our dreams and expectations with a good friend draws us closer. Knowing that our feelings—whatever they are—will be accepted encourages us to open up the next time. Ideally, this process is mutual—not that we reveal tit for tat, but that we each feel free to share when the need arises. We've all had the experience of being "dumped" on: the needy friend who calls only when she's distraught and expects us to be a willing receptacle for all her emotional baggage. We hang up feeling used and angry, knowing that such a self-absorbed "friend" probably would not be there for us were the tables turned.

Actively Listening

To be able to open up, we need to feel accepted and heard. We want the other person to be fully present with us, not mentally writing her grocery list or drifting off into her own thoughts. We convey our presence and our concern by listening actively and empathetically and then by responding sympathetically. Say a friend says, "I'm sorry I missed your birthday this year." A sympathetic reply would be, "Don't worry. I know you're busy," while a judgmental response would be, "How would you feel if I forgot your birthday?"

The judgmental response comes across as critical and would put anyone on the defensive. You're not likely to open up if you must be on guard. Unlike empathy, which helps us connect to a friend, defensiveness creates barriers. When we feel judged, we can't relax or trust the other person. Our energy goes to protecting ourselves.

We can also distance a friend when we dismiss her feelings or deny them. If a friend says, "I'm so angry—my son left a pile of dishes in the kitchen sink again," a sympathetic response would be: "That *is* upsetting. Kids can be so selfish." A dismissive response would be: "Oh, don't let it bother you. What's the big deal?"

The last statement belittles a friend's emotions and makes her feel as though there's something wrong with *her* for feeling the way she does. Because she doesn't feel accepted or understood, she'll probably hesitate before sharing her feelings again.

Saying the Words

When we tell our friends how we feel about them and the friendship, we increase the trust level and further cement our connection. When a good friend said to me, "I want to grow old with you," I felt much more secure in our relationship. Even though we have had differences from time to time, her statement told me that she would hang in for the long haul. The knowledge that she wanted to be friends for life made me feel totally accepted. I responded with "I want to grow old with you, too." I had always *sensed* she genuinely cared about me, but by acknowledging aloud our commitment to each other and to the friendship, we solidified our bond.

In contrast, Meg, a forty-nine-year-old married woman, told

me, "I don't know the level of my importance to my friends because it's never stated. I'm always assuming, guessing, getting indirect feedback." Even with her long-standing friendships, she
doesn't know where she stands. Imagine the anxiety this creates.
Meg did, however, get an inkling of her friend Maria's attachment
when she revealed that she was thinking of leaving her husband.
"When someone confides in me, it's a gift. It says 'I trust you,' "
Meg says. "That's one way of showing commitment to the relationship."

Of course, Meg could offer an affirmation of their relationship
first. She could say, "Our friendship matters to me" or "You're
important to me" or "I value our relationship." But doing so requires taking a risk: Meg doesn't know whether Maria will respond in kind. It's frightening to expose your feelings not
knowing how they'll be received. A positive response could solid-
ify a friendship that feels tentative and pave the way for a deeper
connection. On the other hand, if Maria did not reciprocate with
a comment, such as "I care about you, too," Meg would probably
feel deflated and rejected—at least momentarily. But if she could
put Maria's response in perspective, Meg would realize that she
now knows her status. This information could free her to invest
her energy in more mutual relationships.

If you don't feel comfortable expressing your commitment to
a friendship in broad terms, you can use a specific instance to
show your appreciation for a friend or her thoughtfulness. When
Melissa poured her heart out to Judy about her daughter's new
boyfriend, the next day Melissa sent her a note that said simply,
"Thank you for being such a wonderful friend to me."

Being There

Our friendships grow stronger when we tell each other that we care, just as our children blossom when we say we love them or are proud of them. But often our actions communicate louder than our words. Being present when a friend is experiencing a difficult time, going through a transition, or celebrating a milestone enhances a friendship. Many of us do this naturally by now, but a number of women, who considered themselves novices in this area, had to learn from their friends.

"I've watched other people," Dana told me. "I have a friend from Seattle who has shown me a lot about friendship. When I moved from Chicago to St. Louis, she came to Chicago, moved me down and set up my entire kitchen, and left. That was astounding to me! I learned growing up you don't even do that for a family member. Everyone is on their own unless it's a crisis. You don't take advantage of people and they won't take advantage of you. When I see my friends do things like that for me, I watch. I had to be taught by my friends. It was a long time before I reciprocated at that level."

Sandy's best friend served as her role model, too. "I learned how to be a giving friend from watching how she would give to me," Sandy recalls. "I would think, 'Oh, this feels so nice. Now I know what to do.' For example, when I sounded sad on the phone, she'd say, 'I'm coming over.' I didn't think about doing those things, and now I can do that, too."

Alma and her two best friends try to be present for special events in each other's lives. But if they can't attend, no one holds a grudge. When Alma served as chair of Women's Spirituality Day at her church, her two pals sat in the third row that Sunday morning, even though neither attends her church regularly. She recalls, "They said, 'When you're the chair, we're going to be there for you.' So I looked out on the congregation, and there they were. That made me feel just really good."

When Barbara went through her divorce, it soon became apparent who was a true friend. "There's a variety of ways to be with people in the sense of really *being* with them. Some people will make sure that you're included in a dinner party. Then some will check in with you and others will do something special— invite you to the mountains for the day," she says. "They just do it in a variety of ways, but all of them are equally important and nurturing. But everybody does do it in her way."

Keeping in Touch

Much as we'd like to be there for each other, it's not always possible because of other commitments and obligations. But we *can* keep in touch. For many of us, talking on the telephone is a way of life. Yet a lot of women find it difficult to pick up the phone. And they're plagued with guilt for not keeping in touch. In fact, they see this shortcoming as a serious crime, an indication that they're not a good-enough friend.

Nina, a fifty-four-year-old nurse, is typical of several women I interviewed. "I've always felt that I was not a good friend just because I don't call on the telephone. I have to write it down someplace—'Call so-and-so'—because I just don't like to talk on the phone," she says. "I don't know how other people consider me, but I don't think I'm a good friend. I don't work at it hard enough. When I'm with people, I'm a very good listener and I give good counsel. We have fun together. But in terms of nurturing friendships in the times between—with the phone or a note— those little things need attention."

What prevents women from keeping in touch? Betsy explains

her reasons. "I'm going through a period now where I feel my friends are 'out there' but I can't access them enough. I think it's because we are so busy with our children's families and we all work. By the time we get home, we're tired and tired of talking on the phone. I think every day when I get home, 'I want to call X, Y, and Z.' And then I think, 'Do I have the energy? And does she want to talk?' So then the weekend comes and if we don't have plans to see somebody, I say, 'Well, she's with her family' or 'She's doing this or that.' So suddenly I'm aware of this distance."

It *is* challenging to juggle work, family, and other interests as well as our friends. Yet women who do make time to keep in touch know that those "checking in" phone calls nourish their friendships. Helene makes a concerted effort to touch base with her close friends, particularly Jackie, who withdraws when something is wrong. She can go for days without seeing or calling anyone. Helene says, "I know that about her. She knows that I know it, and I'll come in after her. But if I get lazy or complacent, she might stay in there, and it might be even harder when I do connect with her."

Helene continues, "Jackie rarely calls. She knows I'll call. It's not that I'm a good person, because when I call, I'll always begin with, 'Okay, how long were you going to wait this time?' She'll laugh. At the end of our conversation, she'll always say, 'Helene, thanks for calling. I can always count on you.' I used to think, 'I wish she would just pick up the phone.' One day we did talk about it. She said, 'When I need to talk is when I can least talk, and unless somebody knocks on the door . . .' "

Helene understands Jackie and accepts her. She wishes Jackie would call her, but she values their friendship for other reasons. "She has come through for me in so many wonderful ways that if I were to call her and say, 'I need . . .' she'd be there. She just needs cues," Helene says.

Another aspect of keeping in touch involves following up when you know a friend has a job interview, a medical procedure, a blind date, or an important meeting. It's a matter of phoning and simply asking, "How'd it go?" Although this seems so basic to many of us, everyone doesn't do it comfortably or naturally. Susan agonized over a presentation for work one morning and called Kim for advice. The following day Kim called her to ask how it went. Kim recalls, "That's not a big thing, but she was surprised. When I do nice things for people who are not used to having good friends, they can't believe I do it. It's not so hard to do, but a lot of people have no idea of what it looks like to be available to another person."

In this age of technology, there are other ways to keep in touch if picking up the telephone is difficult for you. Consider using e-mail to stay connected—a painless way to contact friends all over the country or even in the same town. You can write at any time of the day or night, you control the length of your message, and you don't have to worry about getting involved in time-consuming phone calls.

Creating Rituals

A broken dishwasher on Thanksgiving eve. A clash with your sister. A hot flash during your presentation for the boss. We talk about this stuff with our friends every day. Talking binds us, but *experiencing* life together connects us in a deeper way. If your best friend lives across the country, you know that the nature of your bond differs considerably from the tie with a friend who lives nearby whom you see all the time. With long-distance friend-

ships—valuable for their own reasons—we miss sharing the minutiae of each other's lives.

"I think it's important that you experience life together. I mean
that when you meet somebody for lunch, you ask how's it going
and then you report. 'This is what's happening with this one . . .'
Then the other person does the same thing—as opposed to going
to a play together, feeding the homeless, or planting flowers together. That's what bonds people," insists Meryl, who considers
herself a friendship maven. "The best friendships happen because
of shared passions or interests. It's a combination of slowing down
and taking the time to do something together."

How true. When you reflect on the highlights of your friendships, what crops up? You probably remember intimate conversations shared over coffee or lunch. But if you dig deeper, the
times you shared an activity will probably stand out. Hiking in
the mountains together, rowing on the river, cooking for AIDS
patients, browsing through antique shops, walking on the beach.
The whole gestalt of that moment comes back to you: the smell
of the salt air, the honking of the seagulls, the lapping of the
waves, the feel of wet sand under your feet. Ordinary moments,
cherished because we shared them with a close friend.

Such moments become even more significant when we commemorate them with rituals. "Rituals surround us and offer opportunities to make meaning from the familiar and the mysterious
at the same time," say Evan Imber-Black, Ph.D., and Janine Roberts, Ed.D., authors of *Rituals for Our Times*. "This familiarity
provides anchor points to help us make transitions into the un-
known such as turning a year older, or becoming a married person. Rituals bestow protected time and space to stop and reflect
on life's transformations. They engage us with their unique combination of habit and intrigue."[1]

Every year on her birthday, Betsy spends the day with two

friends who share the same birthday—one, three years younger, and the other, two years older. "We're close through the year, but on that one day we really connect as soul mates," she says. They go out for a leisurely lunch and then take a long stroll along the river. "We talk about where we are in life and what feeds us, what's meaningful to us. We talk about those other days when we were going through something difficult and how lucky we are that we came through that, happy and settled. And what life was like for us back then, and how it's better to be where we are now," Betsy says. "I tell them, 'I know you're there for me. I'm there for you. Let's just talk about what this year's been and where we hope to be.' It's just a real important watershed to me. The day feels really good."

Many other women also told me that they make a point of celebrating a friend's birthday with a gourmet meal, a day at a spa, or a theater outing in the city. Christine honors special days by giving homemade gifts. "I knit sweaters, cross-stitch Christmas tree ornaments or breadbasket liners—whatever I think my friend would like," she says. "That's one of the ways I show I care about someone. That's a big thing I do. They are usually the kind of gifts that take me a long time to get ready, and I'll usually include a card that says something like 'Every stitch is filled with memories of our friendship.' "

These familiar, long-standing rituals can make turning fifty or sixty sweeter. At midlife, though, many of us experience life-cycle transitions in ways we never imagined. Rituals can help us gain control of these events and heal, so we can move on. Consider Sarah, a San Francisco massage therapist. In the year before she turned fifty, her husband and father died and her only daughter left to attend college on the East Coast. Coping with so many losses at once left Sarah devastated. Yet she wanted to do *something* to commemorate her big birthday.

Sarah invited her six closest friends over. They all happened to be bodyworkers. In a room softly lit by candles, she undressed and asked each friend to massage a part of her body. Then they held her and sang lullabies and childhood songs to her. The celebration concluded with a vegetarian feast. She recalls, "It was beautiful. It was something I could never reproduce. I only did it because I was at the end of myself. I felt like I was going to die. I was raw and fragile from the losses. So turning fifty was for me a liberation." Sarah created a very personal ritual that felt right for her—certainly not one that would appeal to everyone. She will never forget that birthday or the nurturing her friends provided when she needed it most.

Six years ago when Regina was struggling to reach a divorce settlement with her husband, she invited a friend over who was also contending with a divorce. They commemorated the end of their marriages in a unique way. "I picked tomatoes from the garden, bought fresh bread, cheese, and wine, and we sat in front of the fireplace doing rituals about our marriages," she told me. "We wrote down all the great things in our marriages and saved them. Then we listed all the rotten things, and one by one, we threw the scraps of paper into the burning fire. We felt so close at the end of the evening."

Not only do such rituals connect us to our friends, but they create memorable moments. "It's important to carve out special times," Meryl told me. "Why can't we design a friendship? Design our time together? Do things differently?"

Regina agrees. "My friend Paula will call me and say, 'I'm being a better friend than you are.' We rebalance and reconnect. People are surprised when I say, 'You can have the relationship any way you want. Let's talk about it.' They respond: 'Really? Talk about it?' People love that idea. We're not taught to do that."

In Regina's support group, when the women run into scheduling difficulties or differing priorities, they take time out to reevaluate their connection to the group. They ask each other: What do we each want? What's our commitment to each other? What does the group mean in our lives? We can raise similar questions with a friend when we sense that one of our priorities has changed.

Letting Go

At midlife a lot of women find they become truer to themselves. If that happens, it's easier for them to let others know who they really are. They feel freer to surround themselves with people who nourish them and develop less tolerance for those who sap their energy or give little back. Sometimes, however, that means letting go of certain friends.

While it's never easy to end a friendship, it becomes especially challenging when we must sever a long-term bond. We feel guilty and sad when we must give up a friendship, and yet, say psychotherapists Luise Eichenbaum and Susie Orbach, "For many of us, moving on to new things and saying goodbye to old friends is positive, especially where we have felt trapped in relationships that are unbalanced, draining or only dutiful."[2]

But even when we recognize the necessity and the value of ending a friendship, we don't know how to do it. When a love affair ends we can say that it mattered while it lasted but we knew it couldn't endure, or we can simply enjoy it but regret its limitations. "But no such language enters discussions on friendship," say Eichenbaum and Orbach. "We either feel guilt that we have abandoned a friend or anger that we have been left."[3]

As we've seen throughout this book, women derive much of their identity and sense of well-being from their involvement in relationships. Because friendships contain elements of the mother-daughter bond, when we truly connect with a friend, she almost becomes a part of ourselves. Consequently, "the loss or shifting of a close friendship can stir up, consciously or unconsciously, the pain and anger women can feel about disappointing aspects of their relationship with their mothers," say Eichenbaum and Orbach.[4] The process of ending a friendship carries echoes from the distant past.

A mutual parting, however, lessens some of these feelings. Dana and a college friend drifted apart recently when they both realized they operated under very different value systems. "She was so dishonest. She was living this lie of a life. She would lie to all her boyfriends and come and tell me about it and want me to joke with her," Dana recalls. "I didn't want to be closely connected with someone who didn't value honesty and being straight. We didn't have much in common anymore. College was just fun and games. She lied a lot in college, too, but it was amusing then. It stopped being fun. Our growing apart was mutual."

If all separations were mutual, like Dana's, they would not be so complicated. But usually when friends split, the relationship has fizzled out for just one of the pair. At midlife, friendship duos typically separate because one of the partners has changed, generally the one who wants out. Among the women I interviewed, about half of those who severed a tie did so because she wanted to shed a needy friend. The woman who has grown psychologically will no longer tolerate a self-absorbed, neurotic, or narcissistic friend, and refuses to be used and abused any longer. She wants a more mature, enriching relationship. We saw this situation in chapter 4 when Cindy developed the strength to take responsibility for herself and could no longer listen to her friend Laura constantly complain about being a victim.

Life circumstances can change, too: a divorcee or widow often begins moving in different circles from her long-married friends. Occasionally a clash in values or a betrayal occurs at this stage. But the other most common scenario that creates divisions at mid-life occurs when a woman has expanded into new areas—creative, spiritual, educational, or vocational—while her friend has not. The more evolved friend either has formed new friends who support her development or wants a different kind of connection with her old friends.

If you've grown apart from an old friend, you must decide whether to try to resuscitate the friendship, salvage it in some form, or sever ties altogether.

Resuscitation Attempts

If you sense that an old friend has deserted you, you can try to revitalize your original connection. "The first step toward salvaging a close or best friendship that is fading . . . is to recognize that this friendship requires your attention," says sociologist Jan Yager, Ph.D., author of *Friendshifts*. She notes that often we take long-standing friendships for granted until it's too late. Because we feel secure, we don't put the time or energy into calling or getting together[5]—until we see a distressing signal: a lack of warmth, an obvious slight, or an out-and-out rejection.

Once you recognize a problem exists, you must decide whether to confront your friend or let things ride and see what happens.[6] Your decision will depend on the nature of your relationship and your sense of what would be effective. "You don't have to address every single issue that comes along," says Harriet Lerner, author of *The Dance of Anger*. "There are things that you can let go, and a week later they don't seem like such a big deal. There are other things that are important to talk about, but you don't have to process every single thing with everybody."

Thus, Lerner says, you might call a friend who has been aloof and say, "I feel like you've been distant lately. Do you agree? Is something going on?" With another, you might simply arrange to meet each other, then see what happens when you spend time together—without mentioning your concerns.

Paula Hardin, Ph.D., director of Midlife Consulting Services, has similar advice. "If the friendship wasn't working, I might give it a little space and let it die a natural death. Or perhaps I'd try to make my own 'I' statements and talk to her, saying, 'I'm feeling this about our relationship' or 'I'm not feeling good about what's happening.' Then I'll see what comes back to me." Take responsibility for your own feelings, Hardin suggests, but don't accuse your friend—that would put her on the defensive.

Salvaging Bits and Pieces

As we evolve, so do our needs and expectations of friendship. Sometimes we choose to accept a limited version of the bond rather than abandoning it entirely. Marlene, a clinical social worker, and her friend Judith raised their children together and took family vacations together for years. But in the last decade their lives have taken different courses. Marlene told me, "I remember those days with great joy. We were drinking pretty heavily back then, and she still is. I pulled away from that. But when one of her kids gets married, we're still invited. I go and have a couple glasses of wine, so we're back in the old dynamics, which is so fun and I love her, but it doesn't work for me on a more steady basis," she says.

"But I've never discussed this with her. In my opinion, she's too defensive and wants to stay with her lifestyle and doesn't want to grow and look at things. I accept what we had: a history and a lot of fun. The rest I let go. *Now* what we have is enjoying a couple glasses of wine together and getting giddy, but that's about the limit."

Marlene feels comfortable holding on to a fragment of her friendship with Judith, but she has abandoned another friend altogether, whom she felt close to throughout her forties. "Our value systems were more similar then, but she doesn't have a profession, doesn't work like I do," she says. "She's more interested in getting face-lifts and trying to stay young, and that doesn't interest me. I want to look good, but I don't want to spend time on that. I have a thriving practice that I love. I do that instead."

If you feel you've outgrown someone, as Marlene did, and can no longer be with her in the same way, Hardin suggests you set boundaries for your interactions. You might meet her for lunch at a restaurant and give her only an hour. "Life is short," she says. "How much time do you want to give when something isn't working? How important is it to you? Then you have to make your choices. If this is really important, then you keep on working with it. If it isn't, give it some space. See if something else will emerge in two years."

Deciding to terminate a long-standing friendship doesn't mean that it had no value. Even though it no longer works for you, do not dismiss the friendship out of hand. Remind yourself that it mattered at an earlier time, when you were at a different stage of development. Marlene recognized the significance of the history and the fun she shared with Judith, even though they enjoy totally different lifestyles today.

Valuing past friendships and putting them in perspective justifies them and validates our lives. There's no reason to think we wasted years of our lives with a particular friend. Meryl, who used to feel that she had to hold on to every relationship no matter what, recently let go of a longtime friend. "I really love what we had when we were close. We went through a lot of different things together," she told me. "I still really care about her, but it doesn't seem that we're in sync now and that's okay. It would have never been okay with me in the past, but since I've turned fifty I realize that you have phases in your life and I'm in a different phase from her right now."

Becoming more philosophical, she adds, "Moving along in life and changing and growing and connecting and then separating from people is very natural. You meet people at different times and you bond with them differently. They help you and you help them. You may separate completely or rediscover each other. That's not necessarily a loss, but it's a change."

When we feel good about ourselves at midlife, we don't feel compelled to preserve friends—at any cost. We would like them in our lives, but if it means compromising our values or our sense of self, we may need to let them go. At a younger age, when we ourselves were needier, we may have clung to certain friends for the wrong reasons—perhaps they made us look good or improved our status. Today we choose friendships that nourish us and enhance our lives.

Bailing Out

"Mom, you don't have to maintain friendships that are unhappy and don't help you grow," **Rita**'s twenty-five-year-old son told her. These words of wisdom gave Rita the permission she needed to sever ties with several friends from whom she had grown apart. In her late forties, Rita realized she had strayed from the values she cherished growing up. She told me, "All of a sudden I got caught up in materialistic things, growing financially. It was really bogging me down. Some of my friends became so involved with that stuff that I couldn't communicate with them. They just were so focused on the media, the newspaper, society, and all that was going on *outside* them rather than *inside* them," she recalls. At first, her own guilt about "deserting" her friends immobilized her. But when she developed migraine headaches, she realized she had to let them go. Her son's words gave her the final impetus to make the cut.

Rita explains what changed for her: "All of a sudden I found that simple things made me very happy—a sunny day, a beautiful tree. I was so connected with being positive and looking at things and saying, 'Wow.' But these people were holding on to the negative. They were complaining about their situation because they weren't where they wanted to be financially or spiritually and they weren't looking at the positives. I just decided that they weren't right for me."

Yet even with permission, parting presented a challenge. Just as women have difficulty standing up to friends and speaking out, so breaking ties can be problematic. "If we act on a want, if we differentiate, if we dare to be psychologically separate, we break ranks," say Eichenbaum and Orbach. "We are disrupting the known: the merged attachment . . . The urge to stay merged and the urge to separate exist simultaneously and create a tension in women's relationships."[7] Thus, the dilemma in ending friendships.

Exactly how did Rita let go of her old friends? "Initially I didn't do it very successfully," she admits. "I have a very difficult time asking for what I want or need, so at first I never called them back, and eventually they stopped calling. Then I found myself feeling uncomfortable because I would run into them someplace. I'd think, 'Please, not one of those tedious conversations.' I'm working on it, and I can't say that I'm totally there yet, but I'm able to say, 'This relationship isn't healthy for me.' "

One friend, who was extremely needy, kept phoning, wanting

to stay connected. Rita eventually told her, "No, I can't see you. I just feel like we're going in totally different directions."

Even though Rita wishes she could be more assertive in breaking ties, Harriet Lerner would not fault her handling of this difficult situation. She told me, "It's preferable not to insult or hurt another person's feelings, so there's something to be said for tact and for gradually seeing less of somebody in a way that is not hurtful. I don't think it's useful to say to someone, 'Recently I've been finding you boring and not as fun as my other friends.' I think it would be kinder to just be less available, and distance yourself in a tactful way."

If a good friend with whom you've shared a long history confronts you and asks in a very direct way whether, in fact, you are pulling away, then Harriet Lerner suggests you try to be both honest and tactful. "I would say something like, 'You know, it's true. I really am putting my energy into different things right now, and that is a change. Because I'm so busy, I've had less time for many of my old friendships, including ours.' "

Harriet Lerner notes how aging mellows us in interactions of this kind. "When I was younger, I thought that timing and tact were the opposite of honesty," she says. "Now I think timing and tact are what make honesty possible in very difficult circumstances. So it's possible to say something that validates a friend's reality that things have changed without blasting her, because in the name of honesty, we can bludgeon our friends. With honesty, as with any good thing, you can have too much."

Dissolving friendships by quietly backing off is a mature way to exit a relationship. Yet some women who do so feel that they lack courage, that they "should" confront their friend. "Being passive feels so phony, like I'm an impostor," **Stephanie,** a single friend of mine, told me. She is fed up with Ellen's negativity and competitiveness and has attempted to end their ten-year friendship for the last six months. "Ellen puts down any 'success' of mine. If I ever tell her about a date that went well, she immediately looks for a fault rather than sharing my happiness. She'll ask, '*Why* was he divorced?' " Stephanie mimics, her voice rising.

"When I told her I bought a house, her first response was that it was too far from the city, followed by a comment that I'd probably meet a man after I move in and want to leave. When I said I'd make any man move in with me after all the trouble of buying this house, she said, 'It's too small.' She hasn't even seen the house!" Stephanie fumes in exasperation.

Stephanie no longer returns Ellen's calls. If Stephanie answers the phone, she shares as little as possible. But she still can't make a clean break, as the following e-mail to me illustrates.

Guess who called tonight? Yes, my ex-friend . . . except I didn't follow through the way I was supposed to. This *is* hard. She was extremely friendly and a much better conversationalist than usual so maybe she knows something is up. I ended the call, but only after forty minutes because it felt too awkward to get away. In any case, I will maintain my commitment not to call her anymore. I offered little personal information which was a start, but it could take another year to end this!

About a month later, Stephanie updated me via e-mail on her attempts to bail out:

As for my "friend," I'm definitely ready to end it, but I just don't have the bad feelings it takes to be confrontational. If she brings up my distancing, I will say something, though, and hope she doesn't get emotional. I think my withdrawal is making her more attentive. She is an opportunist—one of the things I don't like about her—and does as little as she can get away with in friendships as well. But even if she "shapes up," it's too late, baby! <snicker>

Six months later Ellen will not let Stephanie off the hook, as the following e-mail shows. But Stephanie has turned a deaf ear to Ellen even though she may be ill.

Remember that friend I was trying to drop? She has continued to call me sporadically, even though I never gave her my new phone number and haven't called her for about eight months or answered her e-mails. The worst: in her last call, she told me about a biopsy she just had. She might have cancer.

The sad thing is that I will still hear from her again even though I don't plan to follow up (yes, ten years of her self-absorption and selfishness have left me that cold). I say to myself that she dropped off the face of the earth every time she had a boyfriend, so let her boyfriend take care of her now. I surprise myself at how easy it is for me to be callous, but I truly regret sticking around in that unfulfilling relationship. When she calls, I am totally disinterested in anything she says.

Despite sounding heartless, Stephanie vacillated for days about whether to contact Ellen. She has finally decided not to follow up, either by phone or e-mail, on the news that Ellen may be ill. For her, that definitive decision halts the friendship, although Ellen may contact her again. Stephanie has made an active decision. She is not taking the chicken's way out, nor is she passive. Just as it takes years to build a friendship, it takes time to end one.

Charlotte, on the other hand, abruptly terminated a twenty-year friendship with Toni, because Charlotte felt that she was constantly giving and Toni showed no appreciation. Nor did she reciprocate when Charlotte developed breast cancer. "I just had enough," Charlotte seethed. The trigger came when she tried to visit Toni in the hospital following gallbladder surgery. Charlotte thought she'd run in during her lunch hour but couldn't find a parking space near the hospital. The enormous crowd from a nearby antique show had filled all the parking lots. She drove around for an hour searching for street parking and eventually went back to work.

"I just couldn't get in," Charlotte told me. "Toni was very angry with me. I understood where she was coming from, but this was one in a series of calamities for someone who was very needy. After twenty years I figured gallbladder surgery wasn't any different than the heart attack or the auto accident."

Charlotte sounds cold and unsympathetic, but she felt that Toni had milked her dry with one medical mishap after another. Charlotte stopped calling Toni and did not return her phone calls. "Which is cowardice, I admit. But I couldn't face her anymore. She had just drained me over the years with her needs. We all have needs, but whatever I gave I didn't get back in any way, shape, or form," Charlotte says. "It felt so good to let go."

As Charlotte discovered, letting go of a needy friend can be enormously freeing. So can parting ways with someone from whom we've grown distant. Ironically, the growth and confidence we've developed *through* participating in relationships gives us the courage to discard those friendships that are no longer working.

Liberated from exhausting, disappointing, or boring alliances, we can invest our energy into deepening the bonds that mean most to us. And we can focus our strength on expanding our inner circle by turning acquaintances into good friends and forging connections with new people.

Chapter Eight

Expanding Your Circle

"Each friend represents a world in us, a world possibly not born until they arrive, and it is only by this meeting that a new world is born."

Anais Nin

I am sitting at a plain wooden table adorned simply with a small vase of fresh daisies at a little restaurant in Manayunk, a trendy, newly rehabilitated section of Philadelphia, with Kate, a writer friend I've known for about a decade. Over the years we've commiserated about editors and agents, shared our frustrations with freelancing, and even compared book advances. I like her a lot and trust her, yet we've never revealed much about our nonprofessional lives. We always seem to have so much to discuss about the writing business that we never get into personal matters.

About an hour before our lunch date, Kate called and asked me to bring a copy of the book I'd written on childhood and adolescent depression. I slipped a copy into my bag without giving her request a second thought. I assumed she wanted it for her library.

Over Greek salads, we chitchat about work, our careers, and our current writing projects. Just as we're ready to pay the check,

I hand Kate the book. She stares at the cover for a moment and then says, "I'm worried about my son."

She goes on for a few minutes and then with a nod toward my book, I ask, "Do you think he's depressed?" Possibly, she says, and begins to tell me in great detail about her son's difficulties and her own pain watching him struggle. I listen. Before long I find myself telling her of problems my son had at that age and how he struggled to build a more adult relationship with Dick and me.

When Kate and I step into the cool spring day to go our separate ways, the warmth kindled between us stays with me. My heart aches for her. I understand how she feels; I've been there. But I also feel good knowing that we connected in a more intimate way. We're no longer just colleagues. By sharing personal concerns, we set the stage for a true friendship to develop. And in fact, since that lunch, our relationship has deepened.

Such opportunities present themselves all the time. If we are open to them, we can seize the moment and lay the groundwork for transforming an acquaintance into a friend. For some of us, that means conquering the fear of rejection that prevents us from reaching out. Yet all of us have an enormous range of options from which to draw new friends. With a little creativity and a bit of chutzpah, we can extend the frontiers of our friendships and expand our experiences.

But why make new friends now? You're probably saying to yourself, "I'm fifty years old, I have my friends, I'm set for life." Maybe. Maybe not. Friends change. We change. Circumstances change. A close friend moves across the country. You discover a passion for science-fiction novels or mountain biking or swing dancing and want someone to share it with. A best buddy becomes consumed with caring for a mother with Alzheimer's. Or you decide you want more fun or that you need a larger network now that your children moved out and your parents are gone.

Forty-two of the fifty women I interviewed told me they had made a new friend in the past year, although most used the term loosely, acknowledging that they still considered the "friend" an acquaintance and not yet a confidante. But they believed that the relationship had the potential for closeness.

Why expand your network now? It helps us stay young. After age forty, according to psychoanalyst Erik Erikson, we must choose between stagnation and generativity. When we stagnate, we're passive, we sit on the sidelines, we vegetate, we wait for time to pass. Generativity includes all the ways we stay vibrant and share the wisdom we've gleaned in four or five decades of living: mentoring the younger generation, volunteering in the community, and I would add, making new friends.

Initial Attraction

What draws us to one woman and not another? Why do we decide to invest our time and energy into a particular relationship? The story of Alice, the owner of a boutique in San Francisco, and Maria, an office manager, illustrates how an initial attraction, if properly nourished, can blossom into a deep friendship.

"I was taking a lunch break in town and saw this new little shop called Serendipity and went in," Maria recalls. "There was wonderful energy, then I saw this lovely woman behind the counter. It's like being attracted to a man, not in a sexual sense, but I know that her wonderful looks and the energy that she exuded spoke to me. I thought, 'This woman takes good care of herself, this woman is gentle.' When we started talking that day, we both said, 'We've got to go hiking together.' "

From that day on, whenever Maria had time for lunch she would stop in and chat with Alice. "We laughed a lot and learned a little bit about each other very slowly," Maria recalls. She discovered that she and Alice had children the same ages and had both just gone through divorces. Still, it was Alice's "special warm energy" that captivated Maria. "I just decided I wanted to make time for this friendship," she says, even though she was working full-time and spent most of her evenings painting sets for a local theater company. Since their initial meeting ten years ago, both women agree that they have become best friends. They credit their morning walk with keeping them in touch and tuned into each other's lives.

How a woman carries herself, the way she dresses, how she wears her hair, her warmth, her sense of humor—and scores of visible and invisible subtleties—affect us when we meet someone. If we then discover that we share common interests or experiences and believe that the potential for emotional support exists,[1] we may try to extend and enhance the initial connection. Paula Hardin, Ph.D., director of Chicago's Midlife Consulting Services, explains this process: "I see myself as a circle. I see another woman as a circle. We're two separate circles. We meet and there's a little bit of attraction there. I open the door to my circle just a tiny bit and give her a little piece of a deeper part of me. I see how she handles it.

"If she comes back with sensitivity and an acknowledgment of what I just offered her, then I feel like I can open my door a little wider. However, if she doesn't even seem to understand what I've just said, then I close the door and barely peek out again. So there's a dance that starts, and you share the moves. Then she pulls one way and you pull another way, and the dance changes. You have to be intentional."

What do you actually say to someone who interests you? Paula

Hardin suggests you be direct and open about your intentions. "I would be assertive," she says. "If I met someone who I'd like for a friend, I would go up and say, 'You really interest me. Could we have a cup of coffee together? I'd like to know more about you.' If anyone has anything to offer, that's an enticing invitation. Who among us doesn't want to be known?"

When Regina, a divorced psychologist, moved from California to Maryland a few years ago, she consciously proceeded to build a circle of friends. "When I meet someone who I think I'd like for a friend, I say, 'I'd like to build a friendship. Are you interested?' Then we talk about what we want. Together we create that. Most women respond with enthusiasm and say, 'Oh, really? I'd like that, too.' "

Next, they set a time and start meeting. They may walk in the woods with Regina's dogs, go biking, or cook a meal together. "It's very intentional and mutual," she says. "It never happens if you don't set aside the time. We talk of designing every element of our work life, yet our personal lives are so haphazard."

Being assertive and intentional worked for these two women, but you may not be comfortable with this style. You may prefer a more indirect approach: invite a prospective friend for coffee or lunch but don't discuss the fact that you are trying to build a friendship. Instead, let your actions speak for you.

A Shared Vision

The attraction *and* the desire to forge a friendship must be mutual or the relationship will probably come to a grinding halt. That's what Pam and Sandi, members of a monthly book group, discovered over the course of several years. Pam always liked Sandi and decided she wanted to get to know her outside the book group, so she invited her to lunch. They found they not only shared a love of books and reading but had a similar view of the world and the same quirky sense of humor. They both enjoyed the lunch immensely and vowed to do it again soon. Six months later Pam called her again and Sandi readily accepted the offer for lunch. Again, they had a wonderful time. But when Sandi showed no signs of taking any initiative, Pam decided to let the friendship languish. She felt she was doing all the work. While they had fun together, Sandi didn't show a desire to build a stronger relationship. Pam wasn't sure how Sandi really felt about her.

About two years later Pam and Sandi met at a party for a mutual friend. By now the book group had disbanded. As they parted after a long conversation, Sandi said, "Let's meet for lunch." Pam agreed but assumed it would never happen. Two days later Sandi called to set a date. At lunch, Sandi said, "I want to keep doing this." "So do I," agreed Pam. They starting meeting for lunch every six weeks. When Pam was on vacation, Sandi needed emergency surgery. As soon as Pam heard the news, she called: "Are you ready for company?" Pam visited the following week and brought dinner. Although still recovering, Sandi made a point of calling Pam the next week to see whether a big presentation at work had been successful.

Pam and Sandi have not discussed the evolution of their friendship, but their behavior shows that they both want—and are striving toward—converting an acquaintanceship into a friendship. They grow closer by staying tuned into each other's lives, keeping in touch, and following up on important events—all ways to sustain a relationship that we discussed in the last chapter. Sociologist Jan Yager offers additional suggestions to help turn an acquaintance into a friend:[2]

• If an acquaintance asks you to come through, do it.

• Avoid gossiping about an acquaintance.

• Return phone calls promptly.

• Take cues from your acquaintance about what pace will be most comfortable for your relationship.

• Avoid taking your evolving friendship for granted or relying on it too heavily.

It is also important to expand your relationship beyond the context in which you first met.[3] Say you click with a woman at work. You gab every chance you get and usually eat lunch together. Most of your conversation centers on work frustrations and commiserating about your boss. If you want to become friends and not just coworkers, you need to discover whether you share other interests. Perhaps you both enjoy tennis or the theater. Then build those activities into your friendship. If you don't, when one of you leaves or transfers to another department, your friendship will probably evaporate, because you've lost the only glue that held you together.

Will every budding friendship suffer a premature death if the desire to build a stronger connection is not mutual? Not necessarily. It depends on the persistence and motivation of the women involved. May has a great need for new friends. Her best buddy just moved out of town and she wants to fill the gap in her life. She has always admired Nancy, who belongs to her church, and has already invited her for coffee twice. Nancy, on the other hand, warms slowly to new people, feels she has spread herself too thin already, and feels lukewarm about May. She has gone for coffee because she doesn't know how to say no to May without hurting her feelings.

Should May continue to pursue Nancy or turn her energies elsewhere? May has to decide how badly she wants to be Nancy's friend and whether she's comfortable continuing to be the aggressive one, not knowing where she stands with Nancy. Six months from now they could be fast friends and Nancy could be grateful that May pursued her. On the other hand, if Nancy does not warm up to May, they could end up resenting each other and losing the collegial relationship they once shared at church. May needs to proceed cautiously, taking her cues from Nancy.

Why Not Reciprocate?

Nancy and May's situation illustrates some of the reasons a potential friend might not respond to your overtures: She may have a more reticent personality, a full circle of friends, or feel indifferent or disinterested in you. All legitimate reasons for not reciprocating. In addition, lack of time can be a detriment. Most of us work full-time, many of us care for aging parents, and some of us still have teenagers at home. These obligations and responsibilities demand energy. "Creating and maintaining strong, reliable, and satisfying friendships requires the same effort other gratifying relationships require: time, attention, commitment, and care," say psychologists Carol M. Anderson and Susan Stewart, coauthors of *Flying Solo: Single Women in Midlife*.[4]

Carol, fifty-six, the new widow from chapter 5, needs time for herself before she can respond to all the women who have courted her since her husband Raymond died last year. A popular newspaper columnist, he had a wide circle of friends. She runs an independent bookstore and her twin sister is active in local politics, so Carol knows a lot of people from several professional and social spheres. She does not need to reach out to anyone because

so many women have approached her. At this point she gets together only with those women who mean something to her. "I'm
saying to people that basically I just want to be home when I'm
not working, which is true. My therapist and I worked out a reply
for the people who are really pushy," she told me. "I say, 'I know
you really care about me, so I know you'll understand that what
I most need now is time to myself to rejuvenate.' I haven't said
all that just yet. It's a scary thing for me to say."

Carol has accepted the offer of a new friendship from only one
woman, Dahlia, a reclusively shy editor whom Carol and Ray knew
casually. After Raymond died, Dahlia called Carol and said, "I
know you have a lot of friends, but I want to take you out for
lunch. I've wanted to do this for a long time, and I'm going to
do it now." Carol said, "We went out, and she was so open with
me, so lovely, so vulnerable, and so willing to talk honestly that
we have gone for walks several times, and I know she's going to
be important in my life." In this situation, Dahlia's persistence has
paid off. Although Dahlia does all the initiating, Carol has made
it clear that she enjoys Dahlia's company.

As a relatively recent widow, Carol needs to heal before she
can respond to other overtures of friendship. Other women may
choose *not* to reciprocate for another reason: They fear intimacy.
Acquaintances are safe. You don't have to risk too much or reveal
too much. A true friendship is an intimate relationship. As we've
seen, women share their innermost fears and feelings with each
other. That can be frightening if you've never done it. Elaine, a
fifty-one-year-old special-education teacher from Minneapolis,
grew up in an army family as the eldest of six. They moved several
times a year, so she never developed lasting friendships. She drew
comfort from being with her mother, a lonely woman who also
lacked friends because of the constant moves. Unfortunately, her
mother died of cancer when Elaine was twenty-five years old.

"That for me was really the loss of my best friend," she told me.

Once out of college, Elaine's life revolved around raising her own family and teaching; she says she did not have time to cultivate friendships. Today she feels closest to her college sorority sisters. They catch up by phone every six months and meet for a reunion once a year. In Minneapolis, where she has lived for the past twenty years, she keeps her relationships impersonal. "When I go out with people, I just want to keep it light. I don't want to get into problems because I'm with problem children all day. I keep it real social. I have fun with my friends. I can let my hair down and I don't have to put on pretenses. We don't get into deep problems. We talk about politics or spiritual things or problems of the city. But we don't get into personal problems all that much."

Superficial or long-distance bonds feel comfortable to Elaine. Other than her tie with her mother, which ended prematurely, she has never experienced a deep, lasting relationship with a woman. Should one of Elaine's acquaintances try to get to know her on a more personal level, the prospect of intimacy might be too threatening.

Holding Back

Whether or not you desire to broaden your circle, it can be flattering to be courted. Not everyone, however, pursues new friends—even when they meet someone intriguing or interesting. They hold back because they fear rejection. They dread hearing, "No, I can't make it. I have a conflict." Or, "No, I'm busy. I can't go." In fact, *they* are not rejected as a person. *Their request* is turned down: an enormous difference and one that hopefully, at midlife, we understand and don't take personally.

We may not even be consciously aware that a fear of rejection hampers us. One woman told me, "There are people whose friendship I would like to nurture. I meet somebody who's nice and I'd like to get to know her. But I don't do it, whether it's time or . . ." Her voice trails off, sounding puzzled. Another said, "There's one woman I really like, and I keep saying I'm going to send her a note or a card. When she was in town, we went out to dinner. I just haven't done it . . ." Neither of these women understands why she hasn't taken the initiative, nor does she realize that her procrastination may hide a fear of rejection.

. Do these women's words sound familiar? If you've met someone recently whom you'd like to know better but haven't taken the next step, ask yourself what holds you back. Is it really a lack of time? Are you so content with your friends that you have no desire to broaden your circle? Do you feel too emotionally fragile to get to know someone new? Or are you afraid your offer will be rebuffed?

Whatever your reason for holding back, honor it. Perhaps this is not the right time for you to extend yourself. If, however, you now recognize that you are not reaching out *only* because you fear being rejected, then on a day when you feel especially good about yourself, take a bold step: invite your new neighbor for coffee, chat with the fiftysomething woman who recently joined your health club, call the woman you commiserated with in your computer-skills class. You may be pleasantly surprised by the warm response your overture generates.

Just Do It!

To broaden your inner circle, you must be visible. Throw on a red blazer. Dig out those stunning earrings you bought at the craft show. Slip on an outfit that makes you feel great. Then get out and circulate. Have you always wanted to speak Italian but never had the time to learn? Would you like to find friends who share your love of gardening? Perhaps you yearn to row on the river again as you did when you were single. Or maybe finding your childhood sketchbooks reminded you of how much you loved drawing as a girl. Whether you want to explore a new hobby or resurrect an old interest, join a club—for skiing, photography, gourmet eating—to find others who share your passion. Or take a night-school class to further develop your talents.

Check the weekend listings in your newspaper for things to do in your area. Let your imagination soar and see what creative ideas emerge. Volunteer for a committee at work. Get involved in your church or synagogue. Develop yourself professionally by joining Toastmasters. Take a cruise for singles only. Participate in a local hiking or biking club. Contribute time to a worthy cause: become a big sister to an inner city youth or deliver meals on wheels to the elderly. Join an improvisational theater troupe. Take a course in investments or computers. Once you're in a new setting, be open to all kinds of people.

Age Is Only a Number

Friendships with younger women keep us young and "with it." Clothes, music, technology—they know all the latest trends. "I'm sort of the Auntie Mame. They're going to be my age someday and they want to know someone who is still having fun," Barbara, fifty-nine, says, referring to her thirtysomething friends from her book group. "I like to ski and I get extra tickets to the symphony so I can invite someone to come with me. Some of them don't have any money—they love to go for free. I make sure I have ways to invite the young, and just offer my life, as they offer theirs. If it wasn't for my younger friends, I wouldn't be on-line. They say, 'You've got to! You just can't ignore this whole thing.' "

On the other hand, a personal experience showed me how being with younger women can make us feel ancient. As the oldest person in my yoga teacher training, I loved hearing my twenty-five-to-thirty-five-year-old classmates discuss their dates, their busy professional lives, and their spiritual journeys. They knew about the hottest restaurants in town, astrology readings, and meditation retreats. If we discussed marriage or parenting, they listened to me with respect (ugh!). But when we started moving into different poses, I would observe their svelte, supple bodies with envy. After a long yoga session, my muscles ached. I was ready to crawl into bed. My young friends had just warmed up to go dancing.

Perhaps we need to focus friendships with younger women on books or movies or on psychological or spiritual concerns—anything but physical activities. Then we can concentrate on the gifts we bring as seasoned, wise women, rather than on the challenges that accompany aging.

Those very gifts attract *us* to older women. They offer a sneak preview of our future. We can learn how to age with elegance and ease and how to face illness and death courageously. Charlotte, fifty-seven, and Mabel, ninety, have been friends since Mabel taught her handwriting analysis many years ago. Of Mabel, who is dying of terminal cancer, Charlotte remarked, "She's a wonderful, wonderful mentor for what she's going through. I spend time with her and we talk.

"Over the years she has taught me a lot. She is totally non-judgmental. Working with something as personal as handwriting, she knew about my parents and what was going on. But she never interfered in a motherly kind of way; she's just been an example of how to do things. Right now she's an example of how to die gracefully. She's leaving me her book collection, which is extraordinary, and her journal."

Helene considers eighty-three-year-old Gertie a mentor as well. Twenty years ago she told Helene, "Don't fear your fifties. Embrace them. They are the wisdom years." Gertie also encouraged her to cultivate younger friends, as she did. "I'm a selfish old cow who was determined to have friends when I was elderly," she cackles. As her contemporaries have died off, Gertie's connection with Helene has become a lifeline.

Christine counts Isabel, her best friend's mother, among one of the most important women in her life. Now seventy-five, Isabel is a matriarch in the truest sense of the word. "She is fierce about family, fiercely accepting, and fiercely supportive," Christine says. "When you marry into the family or are a close friend of a family member, she's very openly loving to you, too."

But Isabel also has a fierce moralistic streak. Christine's clearest memory of her support for her family occurred when Isabel's granddaughter got pregnant—before she married. Everyone tiptoed around the subject, afraid to tell Isabel about the shotgun wedding. Finally, her grandson took her out for a drive to break the news. When she came home, she roared into the kitchen and barked furiously, "Where's that girl?" Everyone cringed, not knowing what would happen next. Then Isabel added, "She needs me." A collective sigh of relief filled the kitchen. For Christine, Isabel is a wonderful role model: "She's very bighearted and sensible and soft—not in a Pollyanna-ish way but in a real honest way. She helps everyone feel good about their strengths. She's a real neat woman. I like her a lot."

Gravitating to Groups

With the proliferation of Twelve Step programs and support groups for everything from shopaholics to overeaters, many people dismiss all groups as touchy-feely gatherings for victims who want to wallow in their pain. While some groups may fit that stereotype, many don't. Groups can give us a sense of belonging, provide companions who share our passions, and serve as a wonderful vehicle to make new friends. What's important is to find the right group for you.

The women I interviewed who either formed their own group or joined an existing one told me that they've met some of their closest friends in group settings. Although the group usually focuses on a particular subject, the conversation often spills into far-flung, intimate topics. The women at Meryl's monthly book group often veer off into discussing personal struggles related to the book at hand. When they read *Into Thin Air,* Jon Krakauer's bestselling account of his climb to the summit of Mount Everest, they launched into discussing the times they've been in physical pain and the personal risks they've taken.

Martha also belongs to a book group as well as a writing group and a study group. Nora is a member of a dream group. Two years ago Cynthia's best friend invited her to join a women's spirituality group. In her "soul group," as she calls it, they discuss their own spiritual journeys and challenges. "We share the changes we've experienced as we've aged, our faith, the role of dogma, and our differences, because we're not all of the same faith." From this group, Cynthia developed two other close friends.

Ruth Zaporah, a performance artist, also belongs to a spirituality group. Everyone in the group, which is called the Dharma Witches, is involved with Buddhism in some way. Ruth described her group: "We wanted to figure out what would be a woman's spiritual practice. One of the major questions we asked is, What are we, as women in our middle years, doing here on this planet? What is our role and responsibility? For myself I wonder when I will be too old to perform. That's a consideration, because I sometimes feel funny getting up in front of my audiences, which are mainly young people. Who wants to see an older woman up there improvising? It's an issue of vanity: I don't look as good as I used to. My body isn't as tight as it used to be. When do I stop coloring my hair and let it go gray?"[5]

Regina and a good friend formed a women's support group four years ago. Seven women meet every other Tuesday evening in each other's homes. Sometimes they focus on a specific topic, but usually they don't get beyond "checking in." In the course of their time together, they have participated in some unusual rituals to bond as a group. At one of their first meetings, they did a foot washing. "We washed each other's feet and talked about the journey of how we got to this place," Regina remembers. They also adopted a Native American tradition, a holiday "giveaway." "We looked among our possessions for an object that we were ready to pass on," Regina explains. They brought earrings from past lovers, clothing that no longer fit, and CDs they no longer listened to. Then they spread all the objects on a special giveaway blanket and each person chose something. The person who gave it away then talked about its significance. The women in this group have become Regina's closest friends.

To start your own group, pick a topic that interests you: books, movies, politics, spirituality. If you prefer a broader scope, such as coping at midlife, start a support group. Talk to a couple of friends who share your interest and see if they would like to help you. Then each invite two or three friends. Encourage them to ask women who don't know each other so you can meet new people. Six to ten women make a manageable group, but you may want to ask more initially, because not everyone who comes to the first few meetings will decide to join. There's usually a shake-out period when people decide whether they will make a commitment. Once you form a core group, not only will you have a built-in social activity but you'll have a new arena from which to draw friends.

Unconventional Pairings

Deog Keun was a bright, fun-loving twenty-seven-year-old Korean woman who came to Philadelphia to advance her education. She already had a master's degree in chemistry but wanted to learn English so she could get her Ph.D. in the States. She had a large vocabulary and could read well, but she stumbled when she tried to speak English. My mission: to teach her conversational English. Our workbook, supplied by the Nationalities Service Center in Philadelphia, served as a springboard for discussion. At our weekly tutoring sessions we covered every nuance of American life, from teenagers' fascination with blue jeans to race relations.

Eventually, we abandoned the workbook ("It's boring," she said) and just talked. She came to our house for dinner, I gave her beanbag chairs for her apartment, she introduced me to her friends and asked if they could sit in on our sessions. When her mother insisted she return to Korea after we had known each other just five months, I knew, as did she, that we'd never see each other again. We both cried when we hugged good-bye.

It's hard to describe the joy Deog Keun brought to my life. I was helping *her* but my life felt richer. In many ways she served as a substitute daughter for me; I also reminded her of her mother. I realized that we clicked as women, not as student and teacher, because I've tutored other young women and didn't feel that same spark. Whatever the reason for my special connection with Deog Keun, I know that if she had not returned to Korea, our friendship would have flourished for years.

Besides teaching English as a second language to foreigners, you can help older Americans learn to read through literacy programs, serve as a big sister for underprivileged youth, or mentor a young woman at work. Over time many of these teacher-student relationships can develop into enriching adult friendships. You feel appreciated and valued for your wisdom and knowledge; at the same time you gain a chance to learn about another culture and just generally broaden your perspective. These experiences also provide an opportunity to meet other volunteers, closer to your age, who share your interest in giving back to society.

Of all the variations on the theme of friendship at midlife, one pairing especially warms women's hearts: that between mothers and adult daughters. Although I didn't intend to discuss the mother-daughter connection, inevitably it arose at the end of my interviews. When I asked women whether they'd like to add anything, those with daughters invariably described their new and wonderful friendships with them. After suffering through the angst and distancing that adolescence brings, identifying their daughters as friends felt especially sweet. Usually, they said, their daughters felt the same way about them.

The subject also came up when women discussed their relationships with their mothers. My interviewees stressed how the bond with their adult daughters was more open, freer, more fun, and more accepting than the connection with their mothers ever was or would be. One woman said, "It is really interesting. My mother feels that she has a very close friendship with my sister and me, and we have to admit we are close. But I know that the relationship I have shared in the last year or two since my daugh-

ter has gotten to be a grown-up has been one of the most rewarding. I feel I can count on her. In any urgent situation, she
will make me a top priority. We also have terrific talks and a great
sharing of our friends."

Of course, a friendship with a daughter differs from one with
a contemporary who is not a family member. Some things we
don't and can't share with a daughter; other things we can *only*
share with a daughter. To become friends, we must give up trying
to control her and her life and work toward accepting her for who
she is, just as she must do the same with us.

Time and Patience

According to sociologist Jan Yager's research, it takes three
years from the time two people meet until they develop a tried-
and-true friendship. Usually by that time acquaintances are no
longer convenient. They may have changed jobs, moved from the
neighborhood, become divorced or widowed. All these events test
a relationship.[6] The pairs who become true friends have expanded
their relationship beyond the original connection, often based on
proximity and expediency.

"Friendship takes intentionality and commitment," Paula Hardin insists. "Early on, it takes reaching out, reaching out, and
reaching out again. And then being there for someone. We need
to learn how much to do that and to whom and recognize if
anything is coming back."

Hardin's advice sounds like an easy formula for transforming
acquaintances into friends. But, as we all know, the process takes
time and energy. *Developing* friendships requires the same attention and care we devote to *nurturing* the friendships we already
have.

"Make new friends but keep the old. One is silver and the other gold," we sang over campfires years and years ago. We've lived that advice for decades without giving it a second thought. But at midlife, as we approach our friendships more thoughtfully and purposely, the words of that simple song assume a deeper meaning. New pals cannot replace our enduring, long-standing friends, but by blending the old with the new, we can create a rich, hearty friendship stew to nourish us in the years ahead.

Chapter Nine

Befriending Yourself

"I must find a balance somewhere ... a swinging of the pendulum between solitude and communion, between retreat and return."

Anne Morrow Lindbergh, *A Gift from the Sea*

Friends can benefit our health. Research studies show that the support of good pals has been linked to hardier immune systems, fewer illnesses, and improved odds of surviving cancer.[1] That does not necessarily mean, however, that the more time we spend with friends the healthier we will become. Too much commiserating and deliberating—two of our favorite activities with friends—can actually harm our mental health. Susan Nolen-Hoeksema, a psychologist at the University of Michigan, has found that women's ruminating about their feelings can prolong depression, anxiety, and anger.[2]

Perhaps, then, we need to learn to become a "good enough" friend. Just as we discovered how to be a "good enough" mother when our children were younger, so we need to be able to give *enough* to consider ourselves a true friend but not set such high standards for caregiving and devotion that we deplete ourselves. To do this, we need to balance time for others with time for ourselves. I don't mean to imply that our friendships do *not* nurture us. Throughout this book we've seen how gratifying and rewarding they can be and how essential they are for our survival. But occasionally, we need to refill the well so we have more to give to all our relationships.

Nothing restores me more than doing yoga in a quiet, spacious room with subdued lighting. It's not for everyone. I have a good friend who relaxes by playing blackjack in the din of Atlantic City casinos. She is clearly an exception. Every woman I interviewed told me she recharges herself by spending time alone. When we were younger, we felt a need to surround ourselves with people, in part to feel liked and popular. We felt defective if we sat home on a Saturday night. Now, with the stronger sense of self we've developed as we've aged, we treasure the quiet and seem to need it more. "I have no plans this weekend and I'm perfectly happy," a divorced woman told me. "In fact, I can't wait. I have books from the library to read and shelves to hang. I'm redecorating my apartment, so I'm going to putz around all weekend."

Still, it can be a challenge to recognize when we need time for ourselves and then to carve it out of our busy lives. Some women feel selfish when they make themselves a priority, because our culture has pressured them to put everyone else's needs before their own. For others, being alone conjures up childhood fears of being abandoned or suggests that if you're by yourself, you must be lonely. Many of the women I interviewed struggled with these issues, but as they've aged, they've been able to let go of many of these old fears and cultural stereotypes so they could take better care of themselves.

Consider the positive effects of spending time alone. Peter Suedfeld, Ph.D., a University of British Columbia psychologist who studies solitude, found that people who spent just one hour in a dark flotation tank—the ultimate alone time—showed lower blood pressure, higher mental functioning, enhanced creativity, and a more positive mental outlook.[3] While I'm not recommending that you spend an hour a day in a flotation tank, I am suggesting that you give yourself permission to revitalize yourself—in any way you like. You are not spoiling yourself if you give yourself the gift of time and space. You deserve it.

Only you know how often you need to retreat and recharge: whether you need it every day, once a week, or monthly. I cannot write a prescription for what form of retreat will work for you either, but I can offer suggestions that have worked for me and for other women. In all the ideas that follow, you'll see a common theme: the need to nurture mind, body, and spirit. When we feel nourished within, we give to others more willingly and graciously.

Mentoring Each Other

When life goes haywire, sometimes it takes a friend to admonish us and give us a reality check, as Sonia did for **Helene.** Helene, who does financial planning, did not realize how work had spilled into her evenings and weekends until Sonia, a good friend, took her to task. Helene had experienced three back-to-back deaths—her father, a close friend, and her mentor—which plunged her into a depression. Yet she kept pushing. Sonia sat her down and reprimanded her: "Okay, how long are you going to keep giving, giving, giving? You can't solve all the problems. You chose a career where you can give advice and you can formulate game plans for people and motivate them, but you're bankrupt right now. You better formulate your own plan."

Helene told me, "She appealed to my pride, to a part of me that knew she believed in me, and that was extremely nourishing. I later told her that what she did was like saying to me, 'You have what it takes. I believe in you.' Because she believed in me, I felt so flattered."

With Sonia's help, Helene realized that she had neglected some activities she loved while she had filled her spare time with work-related business that had grown meaningless. She decided to resign from several boards she served on and began reading historical novels again. They were small but significant gestures. The first gave her more leisure and the second more pleasure.

"We all fall down and forget. Our how-to manuals get lost. But that's what friends do—they fill in the blanks for you. That's part of the wisdom of getting older. You don't have to prove anything anymore. You hopefully don't owe anybody anymore. It's time to be introspective and take an inventory of what you have," Helene says. "What have you developed? Cross out what doesn't apply anymore. It's like cleaning out a closet, but you can go at your own pace. There's no hurry. It's a quieter pace, not so much because you're tired, but you know it's smarter to do it more methodically than like an animal digging a den, tossing dirt everywhere. That's part of being nicer to yourself."

Time Out

A number of women spoke of their growing desire for solitude as they have gotten older, which at times overpowers their need to be with friends. Spending time alone, they found, enabled them to be more present with their friends when they did get together. "I write more. I read more. I do a lot more yoga," Martha says. "I know I'm energized by being alone and depleted by being with too many people too often. It's realizing where my energy comes from, and that when I'm with [others], because I've been alone, I'm much more fun to be with and more energetic. On reflection,

I see how easily I get spread thin with my friends. So I've gained more of an awareness of where my energies come from as I passed fifty."

Cindy, a social worker who never married, relishes her time alone, too, although she has difficulty explaining it to her friends. "This is definitely a midlife thing, because when I was younger, I would want to go out just to do things with my friends," she says. "Now a lot of times, a friend will call and say, 'When are we going to get together for dinner?' and sometimes I'm just happy to connect with her on the phone. At times I just want to be alone, to read, to play with my cats. I guess it's just a personal conflict with me, because I don't want my women friends to think I don't care, because they are very important to me. On the other hand . . ."

Cindy cannot tell her friends that most of the time she prefers to be alone. She's afraid she'll hurt their feelings or they'll feel rejected. At the same time she has a strong desire to be authentic in her relationships. "This is where I have to learn to be more honest, because a lot of times I'll just say, 'Oh, I'm really busy,' which is being sort of honest. I don't know how to say, 'Look, I don't want to spend the time to get ready, drive to meet you . . .' So that's a conflict with me. I'd like to be more honest with that, and I'm really concerned about hurting their feelings. But there's something about saying, 'No, I don't want to come over for dinner; I just want to be here alone.' " She winces.

As Harriet Lerner stressed earlier, tact and timing make honesty possible in very difficult situations. We don't need to process every single thing with everybody. Would Cindy's friends understand her needs if she told them honestly? Possibly, but in doing so, *she* risks being rejected. They may call her less often after being turned down again and again.

The reality is, Cindy likes being alone. It is her choice. But the cultural messages that insist being with somebody—anybody—is preferable to being alone still haunt her. Once she comes to terms with those, she may be more comfortable stating her own needs.

A Room of Her Own

In 1929, Virginia Woolf proposed the revolutionary idea that a woman needed a room of her own (and money) to write fiction. More than seventy years later, at the turn of the millennium, creating personal space is still uncommon among women and yet may be even more necessary. Men escape to their cars, boats, computers, or woodworking shops in the basement. Women's turf? The hub of the house, the kitchen. Their favorite spot to retreat? The bathroom.

"It's one of the few places they don't feel hassled by children or husbands—a place where they don't feel obligated to do anything but focus on themselves," Mihaly Csikszentmihalyi, author of *Finding Flow: The Psychology of Engagement with Everyday Life,* told the *New York Times.*[4] The favorite mode of relaxation of almost half of all American women? Taking a bath. To find out how the other half unwinds, interior designer Chris Casson Madden researched women's personal spaces. In the resulting book, *A Room of Her Own: Women's Personal Spaces,* Madden says women understand the importance of *having* their own space, but they don't take the time to create it. Yet those who devote an area for reading, meditation, or inspiration thrive, whether they set aside an entire room, a nook, or a special niche. Actress Ali MacGraw retreats to a small studio separate from her house in northern New Mexico. Talk-show host Oprah Winfrey transformed a nondescript room near her office. She painted it a deep yellow and filled it with things she loves: African figurines, photos of herself with each of her producers, framed scripts of her films *Beloved* and *The Color Purple,* and her favorite books.[5]

You don't need to be a wealthy star to create a sanctuary, however. You can set aside a corner of your bedroom like Tamara Jeffries, a Pennsylvania editor, who created a space for meditation by simply covering a windowsill with her favorite keepsakes.[6] Author and mountain climber Sandy Hill pitched a multicolored Tibetan tent on the grounds of her Connecticut home and filled it with found objects from her travels. "Here I'm surrounded by the things that give me inspiration to think and write," Hill says. "These mementos are reminders of my journeys and somehow manage to trigger my imagination."[7]

Madden stresses, "Give yourself the gift of it [personal space]. Tell yourself you're going to spend the next two weeks creating this for yourself. Otherwise it doesn't happen."[8]

Creating Rituals

Rituals slow us down. Whether we're saying grace before a meal, writing in a journal, or taking a bubble bath, rituals offer a break in our routine, a way to create equilibrium in our busy lives and take a deep breath before we plunge back in.

Quiet Wednesdays

At times life gets so hectic, we need to go to extremes to achieve the balance we crave. Three years ago, **Nina,** who runs a public-relations consulting business from her home, established Quiet Wednesdays, a day in the middle of the week devoted just to herself. She saw this as the only way to regain control of her life. "The idea was an epiphany for me, because I'm always into doing something for everybody else. I felt like I was losing myself. I couldn't figure out where I started and stopped and where other people started and stopped."

When she first initiated Quiet Wednesdays, she didn't work or talk to anybody. She had to train her family and friends not to call. "I didn't even talk at all. I didn't answer the phone. I was nobody's mother, daughter, sister, or wife. None of that. I just did whatever I wanted to do. No driving. Just sitting staring at the wall or working if I wanted to." Some Wednesdays she meditates. Other days she reads, catches up on paperwork, or throws pots in her basement studio.

Initially, her husband and two grown sons resisted the Wednesday rules. They badgered her about why she was doing it and why she couldn't be satisfied with two hours of quiet instead of a whole day. "Once I started, I felt like a new person," she told me. "Mainly, because I like quiet. I can sit quietly and do nothing."

As Nina continued to take Wednesday after Wednesday for herself, she felt more centered and more focused. Her husband and sons begrudgingly complied. Consequently, she's less stringent about silence and cutting off her family and friends. On the day I interviewed her, a Wednesday, she needed to interact with her husband and sons to prepare for a trip abroad later that week. But she had already warned them, "If you start getting on my nerves . . . I decide on Wednesdays who I'm going to talk to and what I'm going to do."

Observing the Sabbath

For centuries, observant Jews have honored the Sabbath by withdrawing from the world and spending the day studying, praying, reading, or relaxing with family and friends. Ruth, like most observant Jews, attends services every Saturday morning and spends the rest of the day visiting with her synagogue community. Carol, a widow who observed the Sabbath with her late husband, has continued their tradition after his death. Although some may frown on her interpretation of the Sabbath because she does not usually go to synagogue and sometimes goes shopping, she does takes the day for herself. "All day Saturday, I do observe *Shabbat* for myself, in my own style," she explains. "I don't do anything I have to do, like intense shopping or cleaning or anything that I deem unpleasant, from sundown on Friday until pretty much sundown on Saturday. I wouldn't write bills. I go swimming, or I go for a walk, or maybe go to services for a little while. I look forward to Saturday morning when I wake up. Even if I end up doing a little shopping, it's because I felt like doing it."

Meditation Rites

When Christine was going through her divorce, she taught herself to meditate after reading a self-help book. Meditation helped her achieve an inner sense of balance and clarity during an emotionally traumatic year. It also brought her an appreciation of her strengths at a time when she felt so diminished: "That experience of becoming really for the first time very immediately aware of, I guess, my subconscious—I don't know what else to call it. That I could sort of get behind myself and see who I was and find that place from which dreams and ideas must sprout, that was solid and steady and old, deep within me. I just really didn't know it was there. It was startling and very, very comforting."

Books on meditation abound and there are classes all over the country. If you've never meditated before, try the following practice for five or ten minutes every day for a week.

Find a room where you will not be disturbed. Close the door and unplug the telephone. Sit cross-legged on the floor or up-right in a straight-backed chair. Become aware of your body and feel it sink into the floor or chair. Relax your face, then shoul-ders and arms and wrists. Breathe deeply and slowly. Remind yourself that this time is for you. Close your eyes.

If your mind wanders, don't judge yourself. Let it go while you gently try to bring your thoughts back to your breathing. It may help to repeat the following phrases slowly to yourself in rhythm with your breath: Breathing in, I am calm. Breathing out, I smile.[9] Or use any phrases that are meaningful for you. Con-tinue breathing deeply and slowly. When you feel that you've sat long enough for the first time—it could be two minutes or ten minutes—open your eyes, and sit quietly for a few moments be-fore you leave the room.

Although you can meditate anywhere and at any time, many women find it helpful to meditate in a place that holds special meaning for them. Tamara Jeffries, the editor of *HealthQuest,* an African American health magazine based in Chalfont, Pennsylva-nia, describes the altar she uses for meditation: "It's nothing elab-orate—just a wide windowsill where I've placed things that remind me of who I am, where I come from, what is important to me: my grandmother's cotton handkerchief; a shell I collected on a Southern beach; half of a bluebird shell; a fountain pen that belonged to Daddy. These things mark the space where I can go to sit or kneel, in a quiet moment, to center myself and refocus."[10]

The Call of Nature

The ride from Philadelphia to the Jersey shore—a flat, boring drive—takes less than two hours. When I open the car window to pay the toll before entering the causeway to Absecon Island, I inhale my first whiff of humid, salty air. Instantly I feel an urge to be there. I quickly pass through the commercial towns, and as the road narrows, hugging the rocks that line the bay on my right, a sense of calm slowly descends over me. As soon as I enter our special place—no matter what time of day or night—I open the sliding doors facing the ocean. The rhythmic lapping of the waves, the fresh sea air, and the sight of the enormous expanse of water soothe me, washing away the struggles and irritations that seemed so important at home. Within minutes those pressing issues seem light-years away.

I'm not alone in finding peace and serenity near water. Why do so many people long for a Caribbean vacation? My interviewees spoke of finding joy in rowing on the river or sailing on a lake. Strolling on the beach or walking along the grassy shore of a lake has a similar calming effect. One woman, who lives near the western shore of Lake Michigan, gets up at dawn about once a month, walks a few blocks to a lakeside park, and begins her day by watching the sun rise over the lake.

Women who don't live near a body of water find refuge in other aspects of nature. Hiking in the mountains, walking along nature trails, trekking through open fields, or even sitting out in your backyard on a bright sunny day can be renewing. Gardening, too, attracts many women as they get older. There's something gratifying about getting down on your hands and knees and digging in the earth. Then, to immerse yourself in a blaze of color, breathing in the fragrances—even if you're pulling weeds—feels refreshing. What a thrill to bring a bunch of daffodils or tulips that you nourished from bulbs into your house, infusing it with color and life.

Pursuing Passions

"No flow?" my yoga instructor asked me when I complained of difficulty writing that day. "No flow," I repeated, nodding my head in agreement. As a writer, I know flow. It's that sense of exhilaration, of intense concentration when you completely lose sense of time and place. Hours fly by. You forget to eat. You are totally immersed, engaged, and spontaneous. Artists experience flow when they work, as do athletes and musicians. You may have experienced it when making love, playing tennis, or dancing; or at a dinner party where everyone was involved in an engrossing conversation. Usually we feel a sense of flow when we're doing something we love. We completely lose ourselves and will even endure pain to capture that feeling of being transported. Consider marathon runners or swimmers who push on no matter how much their muscles ache.

If you put your passions on the back burner to raise your children or to advance at work, consider resurrecting them now as a way to balance your life. Think about what you enjoyed doing as a child, in your late twenties, or even in the past decade. Try to remember the last time *you* experienced pure pleasure—not something you did to please a husband, child, or friend. What were you doing? Recall the experience. Whatever it was, if it still intrigues you, try to squeeze it into your life now.

Finding Fun

It sounds strange to say, but sometimes we need to remind ourselves to take time out to have fun. We can become so immersed in a project at work or home that before we know it, we feel totally stressed out because we haven't taken a break for days.

Meryl's friend Stacia, a divorced computer consultant, totally withdrew while working on a proposal for a prestigious law firm. She monitored all her phone calls and refused to pick up if she heard a friend's voice on her answering machine. When Meryl finally got through and badgered her into having lunch, Meryl questioned Stacia: "Are you having fun?" Stacia shook her head. Meryl told her, "I need to have something really fun every day to look forward to, even if it's sitting in the garden or walking my dog. That's fun." Stacia stared at her in disbelief: "You do?"

Together, they decided that Meryl would be Stacia's "fun" mentor. For the next week Meryl called her every day and left a reminder on her voice mail: "What are you doing for fun today?" It became a joke between them, but out of their fooling around, Stacia realized how much she missed having a man in her life. She decided to devote six hours a week to gatherings for singles over fifty. Within a month she met someone she was crazy about.

Of course, everyone has her own idea of what constitutes recreation. Another divorced woman may think that attending six hours a week of singles mixers sounds like torture. However you like to play, find a way to fit it into your busy schedule.

Retreating

A retreat, says Jennifer Louden, author of *The Woman's Retreat Book,* is "about stepping out of your ordinary experience to *listen* and *attune* to your truest, most authentic self."[11] You can visit a health spa, join a wilderness venture, attend workshops at a holistic health center, or escape to the mountains or the seashore by yourself. A retreat is both an open-ended journey and a quest: You don't know what you'll discover or how you'll feel in the process.

Before you go, Louden suggests you set an intention, an aim that will guide your action and keep you in the present.[12] It differs from a goal, which keeps you driven and future-oriented. An intention is simply a question you'd like to examine away from the phone, newspaper, and the people who normally influence your life. Some questions/intentions women typically explore on retreats include: Is this a healthy relationship for me or the right place to live? How can I recharge my creativity? What do I need to cope with cancer? How can I be more comfortable with myself?

In planning your retreat, decide whether you want to be alone or a part of a group, how long you can afford to be away, and what type of environment you find most healing. No matter where you go, bring a journal and pens so you can record your thoughts and feelings.

Timeshifting

Maho Bay, St. John, the Virgin Islands. I am snorkeling in the clear turquoise waters in the bay. The sun beats down on my back, the water streams through my cupped hands as I do the breaststroke along the surface. I breathe slowly and deliberately through the mouthpiece. After about twenty minutes, I come out of the water. As I pull off my mask, I say to Dick, "There's nothing there." Then I start laughing. "I mean," I correct myself, "there were no fish."

I had had a beautiful, meditative experience snorkeling and yet I rejected it as nothing, because I hadn't seen any fish. How often we do this. With blinders on, we rush to meet our goal and, in the process, miss the experience entirely. I was particularly tuned into my responses that day because Dick and I had come to St.

John for a week of workshops with the Omega Institute for Holistic Studies.

I learned something that week that was so simple and yet so difficult to do. I gained a new awareness of time: how to timeshift by honoring the moment. Timeshifting, drawn from the Buddhist meditation practice of mindfulness, means being truly present in the moment, no matter what you are doing. "It means conscious awareness of the present, using all our faculties, all our senses— being aware of what's going on around us and within us as well," says Stephan Rechtschaffen, M.D., Omega's founder and president and author of the book *Timeshifting*. "Mindfulness is a state of being that we can experience at any moment of our life. Attention and awareness are all that is required."[13]

Mindfulness happens automatically in a crisis: a car crash, a bout with cancer, a divorce. We can also learn to experience it every day. Whether you're brushing your teeth, washing the dishes, or talking to a friend, you are fully present at that moment. You're not planning your dinner menu in your head or obsessing over a past mistake. You do only one thing at a time. You don't put on your makeup at a red light, juggle a bagel and a cup of coffee while driving to work. In trying to do too much, we become frantic and create a busyness, which makes us feel important. But we end up feeling stressed out, as though time had slipped through our fingers.

In the long run, we haven't enjoyed a thing. We've simply gone through the motions. "There is only one way to waste time: by not being present in the moment," Rechtschaffen told us. "And there's only one way to make more time: to be fully present in the moment. When we're present, we expand the moment."

Only when we expand the moment are we fully alive. Each time we resist being aware, we cease to live. At midlife we know that we're aging, that the years are flying by. We long to stop the clock—or beat it—to create more time for ourselves and our loved ones. But we can't. We can only live consciously and fully in the present. We enlarge the moment when we meditate. When we create rituals. When we enjoy the quiet. When we pursue our passions. And when we spend time with cherished friends.

Finding Balance

By now we've learned that our lives require careful balancing: giving generously to friends and family, setting boundaries when necessary, and honoring our own needs and desires. Out of this process will come both a strengthening of ourselves and a deepening of our friendships. For as we grow stronger, so will our friendships.

But even with the best intentions, occasions will arise when things don't go smoothly. A thoughtless remark by a friend when we're feeling vulnerable, a subtle slight, a jealous comment.

Our friends don't always understand us. Sometimes they can be demanding, or self-absorbed or insensitive. Our ties to our friends are imperfect—that we know by midlife. Yet a powerful, invisible bond links us to each other. Our friends are crucial to our well-being. We long for connection, especially as we grow older.

As our parents age and pass on, as our children scatter across the globe, as we hit fifty and then sixty, we draw our friends close. They cushion our losses, warm us like a down comforter on a cold winter night. They share our joy and our pride.

With our friends, we can be ourselves. They accept us, flawed as we are. At their finest moments true friends give us what we thought could only come from family: unconditional love. And in absorbing that love and acceptance, we know that we truly belong—at last.

Notes

INTRODUCTION

[1] Brozan, Nadine, "Decades After Midlife Mark, A Frontier for Mental Health." *The New York Times,* March 16, 1998, B1.

[2] Monthly Vital Statistics Report, Volume 46, No. 1 Supplement.

[3] Klohnen, Eva C., Elizabeth Vandewater, and Amy Young, "Negotiating the Middle Years: Ego-Resiliency and Successful Midlife Adjustment in Women." *Psychology and Aging,* 1996, Volume 11, Number 3, p. 432.

[4] McQuaide, Sharon, "Keeping the Wise Blood: The Construction of Images in a Mid-Life Women's Group." *Social Work with Groups,* Vol. 19 (3/4) 1996, p. 134.

[5] McDonald, Bob, and Bob Hutcheson, *The Lemming Conspiracy.* Marietta, GA: Longstreet Press, 1997, p. 59.

[6] Sheehy, Gail, *New Passages.* New York: Random House, 1995, p. 194.

[7] Ibid.

[8] Smith-Rosenberg, Carroll, "The Female World of Love and Ritual: Relations Between Women in Nineteenth-Century America." *Women's America: Refocusing the Past.* New York, Oxford: Oxford University Press, 1991, p. 179.

[9] Schultz, Karin, "Women's Adult Development: The Importance of Friendship." *Journal of Independent Social Work,* Vol. 5 (2), 1991, pp. 20–21.

[10] O'Connor, Pat. *Friendships Between Women: A Critical Review.* New York: The Guilford Press, 1992, p. 9.

[11] Enright, D. J., and David Rawlinson, *The Oxford Book of Friendship*. Oxford: Oxford University Press, 1991, p. 96.

[12] Op. cit., Schultz, p. 21.

[13] Ibid., p. 22.

[14] Op. cit., O'Connor, p. 15.

CHAPTER 1: THE MIDLIFE BOND

[1] Rountree, Cathleen, *On Women Turning 50: Celebrating Mid-Life Discoveries*. San Francisco: HarperSanFrancisco, 1993, p. 166.

[2] Bronstein, Sophie Jacobs, "The Experience of Dyadic Friendship Between Women." 1988. Unpublished doctoral dissertation.

[3] Apter, Terri, *Secret Paths: Women in the New Midlife*. New York: W. W. Norton, 1995, p. 301.

[4] Gilligan, Carol, *In a Different Voice*. Cambridge, MA: Harvard University Press, 1982, p. 12.

[5] Op. cit., Apter, p. 302.

[6] O'Connor, Pat, *Friendships Between Women: A Critical Review*. New York: The Guilford Press, 1992, p. 77.

[7] Op. cit., Apter, p. 306.

[8] Ibid., p. 305.

[9] Eichenbaum, Luise, and Susie Orbach, *Between Women: Love, Envy and Competition in Women's Friendships*. New York: Penguin Books, 1987, p. 167.

[10] Ibid.

[11] Rubin, Lillian, *Just Friends: The Role of Friendship in Our Lives*. New York: Harper and Row, 1985, p. 43.

[12] Jordan, Judith V., Alexandra G. Kaplan, Jean Baker Miller, et al, *Women's Growth in Connection: Writings from the Stone Center*. New York: The Guilford Press, 1991, p. 164.

[13] Op. cit., Rubin, p. 177.

[14] Op. cit., Bronstein, p. 98.

[15] Shapiro, Patricia Gottlieb, *My Turn: Women's Search for Self After the Children Leave*. Princeton, NJ: Peterson's, 1996, p. 166.

[16] Hancock, Emily, *The Girl Within*. New York: E. P. Dutton, 1989, pp. 1–2.

[17] Borysenko, Joan, *A Woman's Book of Life: The Biology, Psychology*

and Spirituality of the Feminine Life Cycle. New York: Riverhead Books, 1996, p. 156.

CHAPTER 2: THE LEGACY OF OUR MOTHERS AND SISTERS

1 O'Connor, Pat, *Friendships Between Women: A Critical Review.* New York: The Guilford Press, 1992, p. 156.
2 Eichenbaum, Luise, and Susie Orbach, *Between Women: Love, Envy and Competition in Women's Friendships.* New York: Penguin Books, 1987, p. 55.
3 Ibid., p. 63.
4 Op. cit., O'Connor, pp. 156–157.
5 Ibid., p. 157.
6 Jonas, Susan, and Marilyn Nissenson, *Friends for Life: Enriching the Bond Between Mothers and Their Adult Daughters.* New York: William Morrow, 1997, p. 298.

CHAPTER 3: CHALLENGES OF CLOSENESS

1 Above three paragraphs, Lerner, Harriet, *The Dance of Anger.* New York: Harper and Row, 1985, pp. 5–10.
2 Ibid., p. 13.
3 Eichenbaum, Luise, and Susie Orbach, *Between Women: Love, Envy and Competition in Women's Friendships.* New York: Penguin Books, 1987, p. 117.
4 Ibid., p. 126.
5 Ibid., pp. 121–122.
6 Tannen, Deborah, *You Just Don't Understand: Women and Men in Conversation.* New York: William Morrow, 1990, pp. 24–25.
7 Op. cit., Eichenbaum and Orbach, p. 99.
8 Ibid., p. 104.
9 Greer, Jane, and Margery Rosen, *How Could You Do This to Me? Learning to Trust After Betrayal.* New York: Doubleday, 1997, pp. 54–55.
10 Ibid., pp. 148–149.
11 Ibid., pp. 156–160.
12 Op. cit., Eichenbaum and Orbach, p. 62.
13 Ibid., pp. 63–64.
14 Op. cit., Lerner, p. 97.

[15] Ibid., p. 93.
[16] Op. cit., Eichenbaum and Orbach, p. 149.

CHAPTER 4: MARRIED WITH FRIENDS
[1] Yager, Jan, *Friendshifts: The Power of Friendship and How It Shapes Our Lives*. Stamford, CT: Hannacroix Creek Books, 1997, p. 82.
[2] O'Connor, Pat, *Friendships Between Women: A Critical Review*. New York: The Guilford Press, 1992, p. 77.
[3] Eichenbaum, Luise, and Susie Orbach, *Between Women: Love, Envy and Competition in Women's Friendships*. New York: Penguin Books, 1987, pp. 185–187.
[4] O'Connor, Pat, "Women's Confidants Outside Marriage: Shared or Competing Sources of Intimacy?" *Sociology*, Vol. 25, No. 2, 1991, p. 241.
[5] Ibid., p. 251.
[6] Ibid., pp. 248–9.
[7] Ibid., p. 247.
[8] Sheehy, Gail, *Understanding Men's Passages*. New York: Random House, 1998, p. 148.
[9] Campbell, Shirley, "The Fifty-Year-Old Woman and Midlife Stress." *International Journal of Aging and Human Development*, Vol. 18 (4), 1983–84, p. 303.
[10] Lowenthal, Marjorie Fiske, and Lawrence Weiss, "Intimacy and Crises in Adulthood." *The Counseling Psychologist*. Vol, 6, No. 1, 1976, pp. 10–14.
[11] Op. cit., Sheehy, 1998, p. 159.
[12] Ibid., p. 21.
[13] Oliker, Stacey J., *Best Friends and Marriage*. Berkeley, CA: University of California Press, 1989, p. 137.
[14] Rubin, Lillian, *Just Friends: The Role of Friendship in Our Lives*. New York: Harper & Row, 1985, p. 134.
[15] Op. cit., O'Connor, 1992, p. 88.
[16] Ibid., p. 84.
[17] Ibid.

CHAPTER 5: ALONE BUT NOT LONELY
[1] Anderson, Carol M., and Susan Stewart, with Sona Dimidjian, *Flying Solo: Single Women in Midlife*. New York: W. W. Norton, 1994, p. 15.

2 Ibid., p. 82.
3 Lewis, Karen Gail, and Sidney Moon, "Always Single and Single Again Women: A Qualitative Study." *Journal of Marital and Family Therapy*, 1997, Vol. 23, No. 2, p. 123.
4 Ibid., p. 122.
5 Ibid., pp. 126–7.
6 Op. cit., Anderson and Stewart, p. 84.
7 Rose, Xenia, *Widow's Journey: A Return to the Loving Self*. New York: Henry Holt, 1990, p. 10.
8 Eichenbaum, Luise, and Susie Orbach, *Between Women: Love, Envy and Competition in Women's Friendships*. New York: Penguin Books, 1987, p. 93.
9 Op. cit., Anderson and Stewart, p. 283.

CHAPTER 6: WHEN ILLNESS STRIKES

1 Berg, Elizabeth, *Talk Before Sleep*. New York: Island Books, Dell Publishing, 1994, p. 17.
2 Spiegel, David, *Living Beyond Limits: New Hope and Help for Facing Life-Threatening Illness*. New York: Times Books, 1993, p. 80.
3 Ibid., pp. 84–85.
4 Yager, Jan, *Friendshifts: The Power of Friendship and How it Shapes Our Lives*. Stamford, CT: Hannacroix Creek Books, 1997, p. 158.
5 Callanan, Maggie, and Patricia Kelley, *Final Gifts: Understanding the Special Awareness, Needs and Communications of the Dying*. New York: Bantam Books, 1992, pp. 61–62.
6 Ibid., pp. 62–63.
7 Sklar, Fred, and Shirley F. Hartley, "Close Friends As Survivors: Bereavement Patterns in a 'Hidden' Population." *Omega,* Vol. 21 (2), 1990. pp. 103–104.
8 Roberto, Karen, and Pat Ianni Stanis, "Reactions of Older Women to the Death of Their Close Friends." *Omega*, Vol. 29 (1), 1994, p. 19.
9 Op. cit., Sklar and Hartley, p. 106.
10 Op. cit., Yager, p. 150.
11 Op. cit., Roberto and Stanis, p. 22.
12 Ibid., p. 17.

CHAPTER 7: DEEPENING OR DISSOLVING TIES

1 Imber-Black, Evan, and Janine Roberts, *Rituals for Our Times*. New York: HarperCollins, 1992, p. 3.

2 Eichenbaum, Luise, and Susie Orbach, *Between Women: Love, Envy and Competition in Women's Friendships.* New York: Penguin Books, 1987, p. 88.
3 Ibid.
4 Ibid., p. 75.
5 Yager, Jan, *Friendshifts: The Power of Friendship and How it Shapes Our Lives.* Stamford, CT: Hannacroix Creek Books, 1997, p. 135.
6 Ibid., p. 136.
7 Op. cit., Eichenbaum and Orbach, p. 89.

CHAPTER 8: EXPANDING YOUR CIRCLE
1 Yager, Jan, *Friendshifts: The Power of Friendship and How it Shapes Our Lives.* Stamford, CT: Hannacroix Creek Books, 1997, p. 39.
2 Ibid., pp. 43–44.
3 Ibid., p. 36.
4 Anderson, Carol M., and Susan Stewart, with Sona Dimidjian, *Flying Solo: Single Women in Midlife,* New York: W. W. Norton, 1994, p. 181.
5 Rountree, Cathleen. *On Women Turning Fifty: Celebrating Midlife Discoveries.* San Francisco: HarperSanFrancisco, 1993, p. 61.
6 Op. cit., Yager, p. 36.

CHAPTER 9: BEFRIENDING YOURSELF
1 Browder, Sue Ellin, "Live Longer and Better." *New Choices,* March 1999, p. 27.
2 Tavris, Carol, "How Friendship was 'Feminized.' " *The New York Times,* May 28, 1997.
3 Buchholz, Ester, Ph.D, "The Call of Solitude." *Psychology Today*, January/February 1998, p. 52.
4 Segell, Michael, "It's Guys Only in the Basement." *The New York Times,* March 25, 1999, p. F11.
5 John-Hall, Annette, "Breathing Room," *Philadelphia Inquirer,* October 2, 1998, p. E1.
6 Jeffries, Tamara, "A voice said: 'What you need will come.' " *Philadelphia Inquirer,* May 10, 1998, p. H5.
7 Madden, Chris Casson, *A Room of Her Own.* New York: Clarkson Potter, 1997, p. 88.
8 Op. cit., John-Hall, p. E1.

⁹ Rechtschaffen, Stephan, M. D., *Timeshifting: Creating More Time to Enjoy Your Life.* New York: Doubleday, 1996, p. 68.

¹⁰ Op. cit., Jeffries, p. H5.

¹¹ Louden, Jennifer, *The Woman's Retreat Book.* San Francisco: HarperSanFrancisco, 1997, p. 12.

¹² Ibid., p. 39.

¹³ Op. cit., Rechtschaffen, p. 63.

Bibliography

Anderson, Carol M., and Susan Stewart with Sona Dimidjian. *Flying Solo: Single Women in Midlife*. New York: W. W. Norton, 1994.

Apter, Terri. *Secret Paths: Women in the New Midlife*. New York: W. W. Norton, 1995.

Berg, Elizabeth. *Talk Before Sleep*. New York: Island Books, Dell Publishing, 1994.

Berry, Carmen Renee, and Tamara Traeder. *Girlfriends: Invisible Bonds, Enduring Ties*. Berkeley, CA: Wildcat Canyon Press, 1995.

Berzoff, Joan. "Fusion and Heterosexual Women's Friendships: Implications for Expanding Our Adult Developmental Theories." *Women & Therapy*, Vol. 8 (4), 1989, 93–107.

Borysenko, Joan, Ph.D. *A Woman's Book of Life: The Biology, Psychology and Spirituality of the Feminine Life Cycle*. New York: Riverhead Books, 1996.

Bronstein, Sophie Jacobs. *The Experience of Dyadic Friendship Between Women*. (unpublished) doctoral dissertation, 1988.

Brooks, Jane. *Midlife Orphan: Facing Life's Changes Now That Your Parents are Gone*. New York: Berkley Books, 1999.

Browder, Sue Ellin, "Live Longer and Better," *New Choices*, March 1999, 25–29.

Brozan, Nadine. "Decades After Midlife Mark, A Frontier for Mental Health," *The New York Times*, March 16, 1998.

Buchholz, Ester, Ph.D. "The Call of Solitude," *Psychology Today*, January/February 1998, 50–54, 80–82.

Callanan, Maggie, and Patricia Kelley. *Final Gifts: Understanding the Special Awareness, Needs and Communications of the Dying.* New York: Bantam Books, 1992.

Campbell, Shirley. "The Fifty-Year-Old Woman and Midlife Stress." *International Journal of Aging and Human Development*, Vol. 18 (4), 1983–84, 295–306.

Eichenbaum, Luise, and Susie Orbach. *Between Women: Love, Envy and Competition in Women's Friendships.* New York: Penguin Books, 1987.

Enright, D. J., and David Rawlinson. *The Oxford Book of Friendship.* Oxford: Oxford University Press, 1991.

Fleming, Anne Taylor. *Motherhood Deferred.* New York: Fawcett Books, 1995.

Gilligan, Carol. *In a Different Voice.* Cambridge, MA: Harvard University Press, 1982.

Greer, Jane, and Margery Rosen. *How Could You Do This to Me? Learning to Trust After Betrayal.* New York: Doubleday, 1997.

Hancock, Emily. *The Girl Within.* New York: E. P. Dutton, 1989.

Hardin, Paula Payne. *What Are You Doing with the Rest of Your Life?* San Rafael, CA: New World Library, 1992.

Imber-Black, Evan, and Janine Roberts. *Rituals for Our Times.* New York: HarperCollins, 1992.

Jeffries, Tamara. "A Voice said: 'What you need will come.'" *Philadelphia Inquirer*, May 10, 1998, H5.

John-Hall, Annette. "Breathing Room." *Philadelphia Inquirer*, October 2, 1998, E1.

Jonas, Susan, and Marilyn Nissenson. *Friends for Life: Enriching the Bond Between Mothers and Their Adult Daughters.* New York: William Morrow, 1997.

Jordan, Judith V., Alexandra G. Kaplan, Jean Baker Miller, et al. *Women's Growth in Connection: Writings from the Stone Center.* New York: The Guilford Press, 1991.

Klohnen, Eva C. and Elizabeth A. Vandewater, and Amy Young. "Negotiating the Middle Years: Ego-Resiliency and Successful Midlife Adjustment in Women." *Psychology and Aging*, Vol. 11, No. 3, 1996, 431–442.

Lerner, Harriet. *Dance of Anger.* New York: HarperCollins, 1997.

Lewis, Karen Gail, and Sidney Moon. "Always Single and Single Again

Women: A Qualitative Study." *Journal of Marital and Family Therapy*, Vol. 23, No. 2, 1997, 115–134.

Louden, Jennifer. *The Woman's Retreat Book*. San Francisco: Harper-SanFrancisco, 1997.

Lowenthal, Marjorie Fiske, and Lawrence Weiss, "Intimacy and Crises in Adulthood." *The Counseling Psychologist*, Vol. 6, No. 1, 1976, 10–15.

Madden, Chris Casson. *A Room of Her Own: Women's Personal Spaces*. New York: Clarkson Potter, 1997.

McDonald, Bob, and Bob Hutcheson. *The Lemming Conspiracy*. Marietta, GA: Longstreet Press, 1997.

McQuaide, Sharon. "Keeping the Wise Blood: The Construction of Images in a Mid-Life Women's Group." *Social Work with Groups*, Vol. 19 (¾) 1996, 131–144.

O'Connor, Pat. *Friendships Between Women: A Critical Review*. New York: The Guilford Press, 1992.

O'Connor, Pat. "Women's Confidants Outside Marriage: Shared or Competing Sources of Intimacy?", *Sociology*, Vol. 25, No. 2, May 1991, 241–254.

Oliker, Stacey J. *Best Friends and Marriage*. Berkeley, CA: University of California Press, 1989.

Pearlman, Sarah F. "Late Mid-Life Astonishment: Disruptions to Identity and Self-Esteem." *Women and Therapy*, Vol. 14 (1–2), 1993, 1–12.

Peterson, Bill E., and Eva C. Klohnen. "Realization of Generativity in Two Samples of Women at Midlife." *Psychology and Aging*, Vol. 10, No. 1, 1995, 20–29.

Pogrebin, Letty Cottin. *Among Friends: Who We Like, Why We Like Them, and What We Do with Them*. New York: McGraw-Hill, 1987.

Rechtschaffen, Stephan, M. D. *Timeshifting: Creating More Time to Enjoy Your Life*. New York: Doubleday, 1996.

Roberto, Karen A., Ph.D., and Pat Ianni Stanis. "Reactions of Older Women to the Death of Their Close Friends." *Omega*, Vol. 29 (1), 1994, 17–27.

Rose, Xenia. *Widow's Journey: A Return to the Loving Self*. New York: Henry Holt, 1990.

Rountree, Cathleen. *On Women Turing Fifty: Celebrating Mid-Life Discoveries*. San Francisco: HarperSanFrancisco, 1993.

Rubin, Lillian. *Just Friends: The Role of Friendship in Our Lives*. New York: Harper & Row, 1985.

Sandmaier, Marian. *Original Kin: The Search for Connection Among Adult Sisters and Brothers*. New York: Dutton, 1994.

Schultz, Karin. "Women's Adult Development: The Importance of Friendship." *Journal of Independent Social Work*, Vol. 5 (2), 1991, 19–30.

Segell, Michael. "It's Guys Only in the Basement." *The New York Times*, March 25, 1999, F11.

Shapiro, Patricia Gottlieb. *My Turn: Women's Search for Self After the Children Leave*. Princeton, NJ: Peterson's, 1996.

Sheehy, Gail. *Understanding Men's Passages*. New York: Random House, 1998.

———, *New Passages*. New York: Random House, 1995.

Sklar, Fred, and Shirley F. Hartley. "Close Friends As Survivors: Bereavement Patterns in a 'Hidden' Population." *Omega*, Vol. 21 (2), 1990, 103–112.

Smith-Rosenberg, Carroll. "The Female World of Love and Ritual: Relations Between Women in Nineteenth-Century America." *Women's America: Refocusing the Past*. New York, Oxford: Oxford University Press, 1991, 179–193.

Spiegel, David, M. D. *Living Beyond Limits: New Hope and Help for Facing Life-Threatening Illness*. New York: Times Books, 1993.

Suitor, Jill, and Shirley Keeton. "Once a Friend, Always a Friend? Effect of Homophily on Women's Support Networks Across a Decade." *Social Networks* 19 (1997), 51–62.

Tannen, Deborah, Ph.D. *You Just Don't Understand: Women and Men in Conversation*. New York: William Morrow, 1990.

Tavris, Carol. "How Friendship Was 'Feminized.'" *The New York Times*, May 28, 1997.

Tumulty, Karen. "Turning Fifty," *Time*, October 20, 1997, 32–42.

Weiss, R. S. "The Fund of Sociability." *Transaction*, Vol. 9, 36–42.

Yager, Jan, Ph.D. *Friendshifts: The Power of Friendship and How It Shapes Our Lives*. Stamford, CT: Hannacroix Creek Books, 1997.

Index